FOREIGN SERVICE FAREWELL

My Years in the Near East

His Majesty King Abdul Aziz ibn Saud

J. Rives Childs

FOREIGN SERVICE FAREWELL

My Years in the Near East

PUBLISHED FOR RANDOLPH-MACON COLLEGE
Ashland, Virginia

BY THE UNIVERSITY PRESS OF VIRGINIA
Charlottesville

THE UNIVERSITY PRESS OF VIRGINIA
Copyright © 1969 by the Rector and Visitors
of the University of Virginia

First published 1969

Standard Book Number: 8139-0261-4
Library of Congress Catalog Card Number: 71-76185
Printed in the United States of America

To

MARCELLE DE JOUVENEL

and

JOSEPHINE HALL

For their encouragement

CONTENTS

ILLUSTRATIONS

FOREIGN SERVICE FAREWELL

My Years in the Near East

Peoples and governments never have learned anything from history, or acted on principles deduced from it.

HEGEL, *Philosophy of History*

I

PROLOGUE

THE summer of 1914, on the eve of war, I was in Kansas City, Missouri, selling Dr. Eliot's Five-Foot Shelf of books. After graduating from Randolph-Macon College in Virginia, I had entered the Harvard graduate school to study Shakespeare under George Lyman Kittredge and comparative literature under Irving Babbitt. My eyes were on the stars and my feet some distance from the ground. Then I was lifted as an autumn leaf by the wind and whisked to Europe, Asia, and Africa—because of a murder in Sarajevo.

To most Harvard students at the time the war was a great dramatic spectacle. Few of us understood its causes, and fewer still had any appreciation of its ultimate consequences. Of all my friends, only Alfred Dennis, a philosophical anarchist working for his doctorate in the social sciences, regarded the war with detachment. In his view it would resolve nothing and leave only ruin in its wake. His reasoning left the rest of us cold.

In June 1915, with a fellow student, I was on a scow in New York harbor headed for a cattle ship on which we were to work our passage to France to join the American Ambulance Corps, when I read in a newspaper that I was a Master of Arts of Harvard. The knowledge would hardly have enhanced my prestige with the cutthroats who were my shipmates aboard the S.S. *Luceric*, which brought us to Saint-Nazaire.

Once in Paris I roamed the streets of that city, intoxicated by its beauty and stirred by the historical associations of its monuments. At the Hôtel des Invalides I recalled Robert Ingersoll's apostrophe to Napoleon and at Père-Lachaise Cemetery, Alfred de Musset's tender verse on a willow tree, under one of which he lies buried.

Then I was assigned to Juilly, where a detachment of the Ambulance Corps was quartered at the old college there. The premises included a lovely park lined by tall poplars and weeping willows, which gave it an air of mystery and melancholy. It came to be surrounded in my mind's eye with something ethereal, not of this world. Over the years it preyed on my imagination, much as does one of Poe's tales. Forty years later I yielded to the temptation to return, to satisfy myself that the picture I had framed of it actually existed. I should have known better; one must never go back. It was doubtless youth and the sense of romance with which youth is imbued that had imparted to the park a fairylike character of which no trace remained.

We were only a few miles from the battlefield of the Marne, where General von Kluck had had his headquarters. A billiard table on which his officers had played was still covered with plaster dislodged from the ceiling during the cannonading. Also untouched were unfilled trenches, hastily thrown up and abandoned by the retreating forces. The German lines were still not far removed. When we drove to Compiègne to pick up the wounded, the dull sound of far-distant artillery could often be heard. Compiègne itself was subject to aerial bombardment. The wounded flowed in with only an occasional day's interruption, when there was a lull in the fighting. The appearance of those we transported was the most heart-rending aspect of our work. Some were so heavily bandaged they resembled mummies more than men. Yet it was not until long afterward that the futility of war made itself felt. Youth does not generally draw lessons from life. Impressions are absorbed which germinate only later on. Mine did not flower until I wrote *Before the Curtain Falls* (1932) almost twenty years later. The tragic side of life was thrust upon us every day in and out of Juilly. To escape it we often danced in the evenings with the American and French nurses to the music of a phonograph. With the world turned into a vast slaughterhouse the lust of life became all the more intensified.

After my return home at the end of summer I taught as a private tutor in Colorado Springs in 1915–16 and as assistant master at Lawrenceville School, Lawrenceville, New Jersey, in 1916–17. During the Easter holidays of 1917 I followed the debates in Congress on Woodrow Wilson's proposal of a declaration of war against Germany. I heard Jeannette Rankin, the first woman member of that body, announce in a barely audible voice that, as a woman, she could not vote for war. I heard Meyer London, the only Socialist member of the House, defend his negative ballot on the ground that the war was one of competing capitalist groups which could only bring ruin on the working class. He would have been more to the point if his comment had been less restricted.

Once war was declared, I volunteered and was assigned to the First Officers' Training Camp at Fort Myer, opposite Washington. Commissioned a second lieutenant of infantry, I was sent to Camp Lee and appointed aide to Brigadier General C. S. Farnsworth commanding the 80th Division. A little later I was ordered to the Army War College for instruction in military intelligence.

One of our lecturers was Captain Herbert Yardley, newly appointed head of the cryptographic bureau of Military Intelligence. Yardley had been a telegrapher in the State Department. With a brilliant mind which was intrigued by the encoded messages he transmitted, he applied himself to the study of cryptanalysis. As one of the few persons in the country with any appreciable knowledge of the subject, he had been pressed into service upon the outbreak of war. His lectures so fascinated four of our class that when he informed us that American G.H.Q. in France had appealed urgently for cryptanalysts we volunteered.

To extend our knowledge we were detailed for further instruction to Riverbank Laboratories, a private enterprise maintained as a hobby by a Chicago industrialist, Colonel George Fabyan, at Geneva, Illinois. In addition to a project concerned with the discovery of perpetual motion, he employed two cryptanalysts, William Friedman and Elizebeth Smith. Their nominal objective was to establish the presence of a cipher in the plays of Shakespeare identifying Bacon as their author.[1] The recourse of the government to such an eccentric as Fabyan indicates the level of American cryptographic activities in 1917.

From there we were ordered to France and after twenty-eight days at sea reported on February 1, 1918, to Colonel Frank Moorman, in charge of G2A6 at Chaumont, American General Headquarters in France. It was something of a shock when he informed me that I was to head the Cipher Section, then in an embryonic stage. Happily for me there was no one at headquarters who knew more about the subject than I, because I knew but little. A lucky break resulted in my being named liaison officer of Radio Intelligence with the French and British, necessitating monthly visits to London and Paris.

In Paris I spent a week with Captain Georges Painvin, my opposite number at the French War Office. His patient instruction advanced my knowledge appreciably and was responsible for such success as I eventually had.[2] As a brief account of my work with German ciphers is in David Kahn's *The Code-Breakers* (1966) and a more explicit one in *Before the Curtain Falls*, it would be superfluous to repeat the story.

Upon the signing of the Armistice I had a telephone call from Yardley in Paris toward the end of November, 1918. He was to be chief of Radio Intelligence on the staff of General Marlborough Churchill at the Paris Peace Conference. He inquired whether I would care to join him as his assistant.

Paris had gone wild after the Armistice. There was one dominant idea, the pursuit of pleasure. Out of respect for the dead all public dancing had been forbidden, but in the prevailing mood the prohibition was unenforceable. Dozens of apartments were turned into dancing establishments; when they were closed by the police they opened elsewhere.

Yardley and I had so little to do that our principal occupation was dancing, almost every afternoon and, after dinner, until late at night. A party we attended on New Year's Eve, 1918, was typical of the times. We began the evening with dinner at the home of an American couple resident in Paris, on the Avenue Bois de Boulogne. We were twelve, and after dinner our hosts announced that they had been asked to see the New Year in at the chateau of the von Mumms outside Paris. It was a large affair and there was no reason, so our hostess assured us, why we should not go along.

The same idea must have occurred to a hundred other invited couples who were entertaining friends. So great was the crush which converged upon the Mumms that when we arrived shortly before midnight we found our host standing on the marble stairway at the entry flanked by two flunkeys in knee breeches, endeavoring to bring some order into the melee. He extended a cordial welcome to his extra guests and had but one request to make, that only those who had invitations should proceed to the sit-down supper for two hundred on the upper floor. The others were asked to remain below for a buffet. He might as well have appealed to a raging sea. The cord had no sooner been removed to give access to the upper floor than there was a pell-mell rush on the part of all to obtain a coveted seat. Yardley and I watched the mad scramble with tolerant amusement before making our way to the buffet. I heard a waiter remark during the evening that 3,000 bottles of champagne had been opened for the 1,500 persons present. It was after six when the last guests left. When we emerged in the courtyard, we found there several ambulances into which people on stretchers were being loaded. A maître d'hôtel was busy affixing tags bearing the addresses to which the hopelessly intoxicated were to be delivered.

By March the life we were living began to pall on us. Emmett Kilpatrick, who shared our apartment, had already left to join the Esthonian Army with the coveted rank of captain. Military Intelligence offered to make me assistant military attaché at the embassy in Paris for one year, with a single task which would have left me as much leisure as I had enjoyed at the Peace Conference. I was becoming restless, however, and was looking for more serious sustained activity, preferably in Europe. Yardley had a wife who was pressing him to return.[3]

Casting about for interesting work which might keep me in Europe, I applied to the American Relief Administration, which Herbert Hoover had organized to minister to the food and medical needs of the stricken countries of eastern Europe. A few days later I had my army orders assigning me to the mission for Yugoslavia in Belgrade. So disrupted was transportation that, to reach my destination, I had to proceed by train to Venice, by ship to Trieste, and thence by train to Belgrade. Even then I was unable to arrive there directly. The bridge over the Danube had been destroyed, necessitating the taking of a ferry.

Within Yugoslavia the situation was even worse. To gain my final destination, Salonika, out of which I was to supervise the child-feeding program in southern Serbia, I accompanied a detachment of British officers in a Danube River vessel to Praxovo, entrained there on a narrow gauge to Kragujevac, and went across the mountains to Niš in a British lorry sent from there.

In Kragujevac I had my first concrete evidence of the hopes which Woodrow Wilson had awakened and of the prestige he had created for the United States. A pharmacist who had suffered the loss of his lifetime savings from the war and was beginning afresh with the slender stocks he had salvaged, upon learning I was an American, refused to accept payment for the medicine of which I was in need. A waiter in my hotel, who was practically in rags, furtively slipped into my hands a package of cigarettes, mumbling that it was his thank offering for Wilson and America. It was the one and only time in my life that I have received a gratuity from a servant. I had been present in Paris when Wilson made his entry down the Champs-Élysées and had witnessed the surge of popular feeling his presence had provoked. Few men in history have built up the expectations he did. So contagious had been the emotions he awakened and so awe-inspiring, I had had to sneak off to the side on that occasion to regain my self-possession. There were few dry eyes on the Champs-Élysées that day.

At Niš there was only one locomotive to maintain traffic south to Skoplje and Salonika. Under repair, it was not available until two days after my arrival. There were no passenger coaches but only box cars, and it was in one of these that I made my twenty-four-hour journey to Skoplje, seated and sleeping on the floor, in the company of two English girls engaged in the relief work.

If Salonika had not suffered unduly from the ravages of war, it had been the victim of a disastrous fire, which had destroyed a large part of the town. Large numbers of Greek, French, and British troops were still concentrated outside the city in barracks and tents. That summer I saw many of them moving off to fresh carnage. A Greek army embarked for Smyrna to reclaim a former part of Hellas from the Turks. A little later their shattered ranks returned. They had been ingloriously routed by forces under the command of a new national leader, Kemal Pasha, destined to rid Turkey not only of the Greeks but of the Allied forces that had occupied Constantinople. In the process he was to overthrow the five-century-old sultanate and to replace it with a republic. I saw French and British volunteers embarking for the Black Sea to join the White Army of General A. I. Denikin in the hope of crushing bolshevism and reestablishing a czar in Russia. But there was no reversion anywhere to the "golden age" of the past.

My work was to oversee the distribution in southern Serbia of foodstuffs for children. Three assisting officers were stationed in Niš, Monastir, and Skoplje.

There can be few more colorful regions in the world than the Balkan states, with their wild rugged crags and their innumerable variety of peoples. This is particularly true of Macedonia and, in my day, of Skoplje, where one might see Christian Serbs in European dress alongside Moslems in their red fezzes and turbans, Albanians in white skullcaps, and Montenegrins in their own distinctive headgear.

The crown of the Montenegrin cap, of red, represents the blood-shed in the battle of Kosovo of June 13, 1389, which subjected Serbia to Turkish domination; five gold threads are the five centuries which have elapsed since; and the black brimless band is mourning for that day. I conceived an unbounded admiration for the Serbs with their doughty character and attachment to their own ways.

To take stock of the needs of the Skoplje district Milton Lockwood and I made a swing around some of the wildest parts in a model-T Ford, going along the Albanian border through Djakovica to Peć. It was a dangerous country through which to travel by reason of roving bands of *comitadjis*—a term embracing both bandits and vigilantes—and at times a trying one owing to primitive living conditions. At night our hearts sank when we were forced to sleep on the floor of our lodgings, because the beds were infested with swarms of bedbugs. By day our spirits rose when contemplating the majestic scenery everywhere about us. Things were not always, however, what they seemed. Prizren, perched on terraced hills with its narrow streets sheltered by grape arbors, was captivating from afar but disillusioning on closer approach to its dust and poverty. It was like those rosy hopes of the future which turn into mirages with advancing years. Insecurity was everywhere manifest. Between Prizren and Djakovica the only signs of life were Serbian patrols, a gun and cartridge belt hanging over the shoulder, a pistol about the waist, and a knife in each boot.

In Djakovica we had our first experience of Yugoslav hospitality. We lunched with officers of the local garrison and leading officials, who had met us five miles outside the town. An interlude of little more than an hour came between luncheon and dinner at the home of Alan Bey, chief of the local *comitadjis*. It was puzzling to find him accepted as one of the leading citizens; I had to conclude that in Macedonia banditry, whether official or unofficial, carried no stigma. Except as servers, no women were present at lunch or dinner or, indeed, at any social function we attended in the course of our Macedonian travels. Their absence was a relic of Moslem tradition introduced by the Turks, which I was to find later throughout the Near East.

If there are any heavier drinkers than the Serbs, I have never encountered them. Fortunately for me, at dinner I had a window at my back through which I could toss unobserved from time to time the wine and slivovitz served us. For Lockwood there was no such escape; the dinner had not ended before, with glazed eyes, he slipped unconscious out of his chair to the floor.

The hospitality offered us at Djakovica, in recognition of our character as Americans and as representatives of a country which had come to the relief of Yugoslavia, was but a prelude of that accorded us throughout our journeys. Upon halting en route to Peć to visit the ancient monastery of Detchani in the mountains, we were shown over its manuscript treasures. When we expressed particular interest in one illustrated on vellum, the monk who was our guide tore out two of its pages and handed them to us as a token of Yugoslav admiration for the United States. At Peć a guard of honor was mounted outside our lodgings and specially assigned orderlies accompanied us wherever we went. We had to abandon the purchase of souvenirs when, upon making our selection in a shop, we were informed that the merchants had orders not to accept payment for anything that we might buy.

The evening before our departure we were the honor guests at a banquet attended by some sixty of the leading citizens. For the first time in the town's history priests of the four local faiths: Greek Orthodox, Roman Catholic, Moslem, and Jewish sat at a table together. At the end of the dinner the Greek Orthodox priest rose and approached the Moslem mullah's chair. "In drinking to the health of President Wilson and the United States in the presence of these two Americans whose country we are assembled to honor, let us bury all differences and proclaim our union as brothers."

Every eye in the room was turned on the Moslem. He hesitated an instant before he arose. "Friends, my religion forbids fermented drink. As a holy man I should set an example. There comes perhaps once in a lifetime, on an occasion such as this, when observance of the strict letter of the law may become a greater offense than its transgression." He paused to take hold of the untouched glass of wine beside his plate and continued: "I therefore drink with you on this unique occasion, in honor of a country to whose ideals we pay homage, in this fraternal association, in trying here to emulate them."

Hysterical applause was the reaction of the assembled diners. Men embraced one another. Some wept unashamedly in the fervor of their emotions; others shouted and danced about the floor. So carried away was the crowd that when the dinner broke up, Lockwood and I were seized and borne on the shoulders of the diners through the streets to our lodgings.

We were awed and shaken by the outpouring of affection and admiration for our country. We were awed by the depth of it and, at the same time, we were disturbed at the thought of the disillusionment which might follow our failure to live up to expectations.

Notwithstanding the deep satisfaction given me by my work— saving lives instead of taking them—and an appeal that I stay on until spring, I was becoming impatient to return home and to take up a definitive career. I offered my resignation and toward the end of August 1919 seized an opportunity offered by the departure of a French troopship from Salonika for Constantinople. It was a round-about way but I desired to see something more of the area before returning to Paris. I had only to write out my own orders for transportation to be accepted on board the vessel.

Constantinople, or Istanbul as it is now known, was and is one of the world's great cities. Its situation on the Golden Horn, its minarets and bulbous domes, give it distinctiveness and exotic beauty. Its age-old importance as the capital of the Byzantine Empire, the center of Crusader struggles, and the capital of the Ottoman Empire envelops it with historic interest symbolized by a variety of monuments preserved from the past.

Going by way of the Black Sea to Constanța, where Ovid lived in exile, and thence through Bucharest, Budapest, and Vienna, I reached Paris when September was well advanced. A major frowned as he examined the telegraphic orders issued to me some weeks earlier. "You seem to have taken a hell of a long time from Salonika."

"Communications are still a bit difficult in the Balkans, sir. I had to come out by way of Constantinople."

"Humph! I'll have to take your word for it. In any case we'll get you out of here for Brest by tomorrow." When I made no move to leave the major looked up at me from his papers. "What is it now?" he growled.

"It's this way, Major. I spent four months here at the Peace Conference and made many friends. I have not had any leave this year. What I would like, sir, is about ten days before receiving my orders."

It was some seconds before he spoke. He spread himself in his chair and glared at me. "Well of all the g— d— nerve. You come in here three weeks after the receipt of your orders and ask for leave!" Then his face relaxed and he picked up a pen. "All I can say is, Lieutenant, I have to admire your gall; I admire it so much that I am going to give you ten days, ten days, do you hear? but not one day more."

In some ways I regretted it. Paris was not the same; no place ever is after a lapse of time. Paris had sobered up after the prolonged debauch which had followed the Armistice. The realities of life had begun to make themselves felt as they do the morning after. None of my old friends were in the city, and without them the old places had no appeal. It was almost with relief that I entrained for Brest, where I was lodged in a camp outside the city with thousands of officers awaiting repatriation. I was three weeks in the rain and mud of the camp before I embarked for home.

By the time I reached New York I had decided on my future career. In my uniform it was easy to gain admittance to the distinguished general manager of the Associated Press, Melville Stone. I almost compromised myself when, in setting forth the object of my visit, I referred to the "newspaper game." "Game!" he spluttered, "Young man, let me tell you it's not a game but a serious profession." In the end he was good enough to offer to pass me on to the manager of the Washington bureau, Richard Probert, to give me a hearing. An immediate foreign assignment was out of the question; first I would have to prove my competence.

The staff of the Associated Press in Washington, probably the most important of all its bureaus, comprised about twenty-six persons when I joined it. At least four went on to positions of national prominence: Byron Price, who later became head of censorship in the Second World War and subsequently Assistant Secretary General of the United Nations; Steve Early, secretary to President Roosevelt; Willard Kiplinger, who founded his own news service; and George Wythe, who later became head of the Latin-American Division of the Department of Commerce. Kiplinger discussed with me his plans for the Kiplinger Service and even urged me to join him, but I was not interested.

I began work on the night shift and spent my time carrying copy. In mounting discouragement I took the initiative after some weeks by turning in some stories of what I had seen in Yugoslavia, giving them a Salonika or Skoplje dateline. Then one night, after reading a number of telegrams from various parts of the world on the international situation, I gave them an introductory lead and turned my draft in to Dean Simpson, the choleric night editor. "Humph!" was his enigmatic comment as he tossed it aside. The next day Probert sent for me. He was a man of singularly few words, and it was one of the rare occasions during my two years under him that he did more than nod to me. "That was a good lead you wrote last night, even though we did not use it. I have decided to put you at the White House. With Wilson as ill as he is there is not a great deal to do, but I want you also to understudy Mr. Hood at the State Department."

The White House was one of the most responsible "runs" in the bureau, and to work with Edwin C. Hood, senior member of the staff and confidant of Secretaries of State and ambassadors, was itself a rare privilege. There was no more respected newspaperman in Washington. When Ion Perdicaris, an American in Tangier, had been kidnaped by a Moroccan chieftain, Raisuli, some years earlier, the Secretary of State, John Hay, had shown Hood the note he proposed to send to the Sultan of Morocco. Hood had not hesitated to tell him that the note was phrased too legally and that he should replace it with a briefer message such as would be likely to appeal to a ruler unfamiliar with diplomatic niceties. "Have you anything in mind?" Hay asked. Hood considered a moment. "What about 'Perdicaris alive or Raisuli dead'?" It was dispatched and became a sensation. So in keeping was it with the pungent diction of President Theodore Roosevelt that the delighted American public credited him with its authorship. Hood's part has always been ignored.

A reporter gains knowledge at first hand of the daily manipulation of news and often finds it difficult to resist the temptation to twist a story for the entertainment of the public. When Einstein called on President Harding, I gave thought to what I might write to color the account in a manner which neither would be disposed to deny. I had a happy inspiration and built a story around Harding's confession of his inability to understand Einstein's theory of relativity. Harding's intellectual deficiencies were widely recognized, but he was not the fool he would have made himself if he had dared to repudiate my story. It made such a hit that most newspapers boxed it on the front page. The New York *World* even made it the subject of an editorial in which I was chided for not having reported

Einstein's answer that he was equally unable to understand Harding's theory of "normalcy."

The incident, small in itself, is illustrative of how reporters create news or slant it to cater to the public craving for sensation. The journalist, and even the diplomat, when reporting events has a tendency to shape his presentation in a manner responsive to the point of view of the public or of his government. Wishful thinking may also interpose itself to distort an objective picture. This was particularly true of dispatches from State Department representatives reporting developments in Soviet Russia after the First World War. At one of the weekly press conferences of Bainbridge Colby, Wilson's last Secretary of State, he read to press association representatives a telegram from the American Minister at Riga predicting that the Soviet regime would collapse within weeks. It was a prediction which had been made so often that Colby was informed it was unpublishable unless he might be quoted. He gave his consent and I was dictating the story over the telephone when Jim Williams, the profane and cynical day editor, broke in on the line. "Stop wasting our time with such tripe," he said. "The AP is tired of overthrowing the Soviet Government for the State Department and then being left holding the bag. We'll carry no more such stories except when based on formal written statements." Yet it was on such misinformation, in the absence of any accredited diplomatic representation in Soviet Russia, that our policy from 1918 to 1933 was being formulated.

An opportunity came to me about 1920 to make public one of the few first-hand accounts of conditions in Soviet Russia which had come out of that country since our mission had been withdrawn in 1918. Tipped off that Colonel Edward W. Ryan, American Red Cross commissioner to the Baltic, had visited Russia surreptitiously with the Esthonian Peace Commission and had submitted a sensational report, I applied to old friends in Military Intelligence for confirmation. Yes, such a report, vividly written and highly interesting, had been received. Would I care to have a look at it? Once it was handed to me, my friend left the room for a quarter of an hour. In his absence I began to make extended extracts. On his return he was uncertain whether he should permit me to quote directly from the text until I presented the specious justification: "The American public have a right to know the facts." This insidious plea has wrecked more international conferences and has been productive of more international and, for that matter, domestic harm than is commonly realized. What I desired was the sensational scoop which I recognized the story to be and I did not consider the possible consequences.

The AP does not customarily carry a story of more than one thousand words short of a war, a panic, or the death of a President. Mine ran to about twelve hundred words. Colonel Ryan had a picturesque, vigorous style and he brought to life what he had seen and heard. A dramatic touch was given to his talk with Grigori Chicherin, People's Commissar for Foreign Affairs, who had served before the war as a young secretary in the Imperial Russian Embassy in Paris. Drawing Ryan to a window of the Kremlin, Chicherin had gazed on the bleakness of the throngs in the square and had nostalgically inquired of Ryan: "Tell me something of Paris. Is it still the same?"

I had expected the story to make a splash, but I was not prepared for the sensation it created. The New York papers spread it under a triple banner headline, and my salary was raised from fifty to fifty-five dollars a week.[4]

About this time my old roommate in Paris, Emmett Kilpatrick, came into the news. The State Department issued a handout reporting the receipt of a telegram announcing his capture by the Bolsheviks while serving with the Red Cross attached to a White army in southern Russia. It was stated that his home address was unknown. I was able to supply it as Uniontown, Alabama, and it gave me the occasion to write what I thought was a romantic little piece about him—of how he had joined the Esthonian Army to attain his ambition of a captaincy such as his father had held in the Confederate Army and had passed thence into the Red Cross. The disservice I rendered him in thus publicizing his activities, particularly the campaign in which he had been engaged against the Bolsheviks, escaped me wholly.

For want of news at the White House during the illness of Woodrow Wilson I had cultivated some of the subordinate executive personnel and from one of these I had drawn the startling admission that the President's state of health was so impaired it was improbable he would ever again play an active role in political life. Joseph Tumulty, the President's secretary through whom news was normally channeled, and members of Wilson's immediate family had been careful to withhold any news that might lead to the inference of incapacity on the part of the Chief Executive. When my story was published, Tumulty was livid with rage and at his daily press conference he took me severely to task without being able to deny the facts.

My war experiences and particularly the evidence I had been given in Yugoslavia of what Wilson meant to the world had profoundly attached me to him. The loss of his health in the unsuccessful campaign he had waged for the League of Nations and the displacement of his high purposes by the cynical ones of his opponents I took personally to heart.

The news of Warren Harding's nomination in June 1920 as Republican candidate for the presidency flabbergasted me. No one took Harding seriously, not even he himself. Some weeks before his nomination I had heard him speak informally at the National Press Club. He had been candid enough to state that he did not consider himself presidential timber and that it had only been at the urging of his friend, Harry M. Daugherty, that he had consented to run. It was all due to his consistent inability to say no to anyone. As a boy, growing up, his father had once said to him, "Warren, it's a good thing you were not born a girl or you would be in a family way most of the time." That he was tragically correct in his self-analysis became quickly evident in the scandals which rocked his administration, leading to the resignation of Daugherty as Attorney General and the imprisonment of Secretary of the Interior Albert B. Fall and the director of the Veterans' Bureau, Charles R. Forbes. That corruption existed among the lowly as well as the prominent figures of the Harding regime may be inferred from the fact that during Prohibition I bought liquor from a bootlegger who transacted business in the basement of the executive offices of the White House.

A few days before Harding was inaugurated I wrote to President Wilson expressing my deep admiration for him and asking for an interview which might enable him to deliver his valedictory to the American people. The morning of the inauguration Tumulty informed me that the President had written me the previous evening, March 3, 1921, refusing my request but thanking me for the tribute I had paid him. It was one of the last four letters he had dictated from the White House.

The inauguration ceremonies at the Capitol were a melancholy occasion for me. Through exceptional circumstances I was the only newsman present in the presidential suite where Wilson was seated, signing the last bills submitted to him by the expiring Congress. I had a post of vantage, immediately behind his chair in the small room in which were assembled Mrs. Wilson, the Hardings, General John J. Pershing, Chief Justice Edward D. White, and a small group of other distinguished people. Shortly before midday there was a subdued murmur as Senator Henry Cabot Lodge entered the room. I have never seen a more malevolent look on the face of a man than that with which Lodge, majority leader of the Senate, regarded the crippled figure of Wilson.

"Mr. President," Lodge began, "I have been directed by the Congress to wait on you to ascertain whether you have any further communication to make before a motion is offered for adjournment."

There was a deathly silence as the attention of all in the room was focused on this dramatic last encounter between the two principal protagonists of the struggle over American entry into the League of Nations. One of the two had been paralyzed in the contest, while the other had been left to gloat in triumph over his defeated opponent. Now they were confronting each other as if in a Shakespearean tragedy: Lodge, resembling a Mephistopheles in the sinister coldness of his regard, and Wilson, surveying the figure before him with Olympian detachment and with a spirit of serenity.

"No, I have no further communication to make to the Congress," was the President's reply.

They were Wilson's last official words. He had already spoken all that was in his mind. He had given repeated warnings of the perils to the United States and to the world of American repudiation of the League of Nations. He had sensed, with that gift given to prophets, what I had seen in Yugoslavia of the hopes which the little people had placed in the United States. Lodge, his party, and the Senate had spoken. The immediate interests of a faction had prevailed over the long-term interests of the country. The President had no further communication to make. He had had his say; the rest was silence. There was left to be drawn now only the judgment of history. And it was to be rendered almost on the morrow.

It was common gossip among well-informed newspapermen in Washington that, at a decisive moment in the Senate's consideration of American entry into the League, Will Hays, chairman of the Republican National Committee, had met with Republican senators to discuss the strategy to be followed. I was informed that he had urged defeat of American adherence to the League on the ground that, if Wilson's will prevailed, it would be disadvantageous to the Republican party. It is clear that partisanship played a preponderant role in the rejection of the League, although it must be confessed that the mood of the American people was then one of reaction to Wilsonian idealism. Wilson had conducted them to the mountain tops, but what they were longing for was a more tranquil existence in the valley.

A few weeks after the inauguration of Harding one of the correspondents attached to the White House proposed the formation of an association of those newspapermen regularly assigned there. The first dinner was held on May 7, 1921, at the Arlington Hotel, with George B. Christian, Jr., Harding's secretary, as guest of honor. No more than a score of correspondents were in attendance. One of the six or eight guests had supplied, for our conviviality, twelve quarts of whiskey notwithstanding Prohibition.

Christian was called on for a speech after the contents of the bottles had been appreciably diminished. With a thick tongue he launched into one of the frankest exposés ever made of a President by his secretary. According to Christian, Harding had never aspired to the office. Moreover, he had never expected to be elected. Now that he was in occupancy of the White House, he was deeply concerned by a sense of his inadequacy. Christian in turn, was apprehensive about his own ability to discharge the heavy responsibilities that had been thrust upon him. After repetitiously striking these chords and wandering around and about the subject, he appealed to the correspondents, whom he described as "the finest, jolliest, and greatest fellows in the world," to stand by him and the President in covering up rather than exposing their shortcomings. Then he took his seat, to the obvious relief of everyone. The next day as we arrived at the White House, we were taken aside by Frank Lamb, president of the Association. "Christian is deeply concerned about the ill-considered speech he made last night. He has asked me to impress on everyone the necessity of forgetting it. I have given him my word that we will."

Christian is dead, as are most of those who were present at the dinner. The White House correspondents respected Christian's plea. There can be no further need for silence about matters on which history is no longer silent. The annual dinner of the association has now become a formal affair, attended by the President. Chief Executives no doubt desire to make sure there will be no more indiscretions such as those which distinguished the first meeting.

Numerous opportunities were afforded me to measure the intellectual stature of Harding. At a garden party for veterans on the White House lawn I overheard a colloquy between him and a blind and legless soldier. "Do you like to be read to?" the President asked. "Not particularly," was the reply from one who appeared to have enjoyed few advantages in life. "You might find comfort in books," Harding continued. "There are some in which I have found great inspiration."

I was now hanging on his words. An account of the books which inspired a President would make an interesting story, especially in the case of one who had small reputation as a serious reader.

"The works which have always given me a great lift and would, I am sure, cheer your own life, are the Pollyanna books."

I scrutinized the President to make sure that he was in earnest. There could be no least doubt of that, and I turned away in disgust. The Associated Press would never disseminate news tending to hold a President up to public ridicule.

Despite the bright promise opened up to me by my work as a Washington correspondent, I had become increasingly restive by the spring of 1921. Probert, bent on retaining me in Washington because of the valuable contacts I had formed, was unreceptive to pleas that he support my application for a foreign assignment. My heart was in Europe; assurance of the brightest prospects as a correspondent in my own country left me quite cold.

When an opportunity arose to apply for leave to go to Europe to write a series of articles for the Belleau Woods Memorial Association, I seized it. Once abroad I could look around for an opening as foreign correspondent. Failing that, I could always return to my job in Washington. But this last was remote in my calculations.

II

A NEW WORLD:
SOVIET RUSSIA

O N RETURNING from Belleau Woods to Paris in the summer of
1921, I picked up a copy of the Paris edition of the Chicago
Tribune. In it was an announcement of a meeting soon to take place
in Riga between Maxim Litvinoff and Charles Lyman Brown to
examine the possibility that the American Relief Administration
might undertake to render assistance in a widespread Russian famine.
Owing to vagaries of climate and inadequate transport Russia had
had periodic famines in the past, but none so widespread as the
present one. Soviet authorities had had to appeal to the outside
world for help.

An opportunity to see something of that extraordinary new world
attracted me. In answer to a letter to the ARA in London, I was
informed that as soon as the negotiations were concluded I could
count on being engaged for the work in the light of my previous
experience with the organization in Yugoslavia. George Wythe, an
old colleague on the Associated Press, was now commercial attaché
in Vienna and had invited me to visit him. I decided to accept and
await there the expected call. At the same time I could make the
acquaintance of a city whose charms were reputed to be second
only to those of Paris. A few days later on a Sunday at the end of
August George and I were lunching in the garden of his country
place at Baden when the telephone rang. The American Legation
reported the receipt of a telegram for me from the ARA in London,
ordering me to report at once to Riga preparatory to entering Soviet
Russia with the mission. The entire course of my life was changed
by that appointment.

Upon reaching Riga I learned of the presence there of two men
whose lives had touched mine: Emmett Kilpatrick, whom I had
known in Paris, and Colonel Ryan, whom I had never met. I was
aware I had unwittingly shaped the destiny of the latter, but it was

only after I had come face to face with Emmett that I learned of
how I had been an unintentional instrument in molding his fate. He
had just been released from prison in Soviet Russia, with other
Americans, under the terms of the Riga Agreement concluded
between Litvinoff and Brown. When we met for lunch I hardly
recognized him. Instead of his old boyish self he was haggard,
nervous, and distraught. As we talked his eyes roved about like those
of a hunted animal. There was every reason for the changes I found
in him: he had just emerged from months of solitary confinement in
the dread Lubianka Prison in Moscow.

After joining the Esthonian Army, he had taken part in several
engagements. Then peace was concluded. Still in search of adventure he was assigned by the American Red Cross to Wrangel's
White Army in southern Russia. There one day he had been cut off
and taken prisoner. In the beginning he was given freedom of
movement. He was even permitted to seek out General Semen
Budenny, famous cavalry leader, who received him cordially. Emmett told him that he admired him because of his great resemblance
to General Nathan B. Forrest, the Confederate commander.

Emmett was eventually ordered to report to Moscow, where a
questionnaire was given him to complete. One of the questions was
whether he had ever taken up arms against Soviet Russia. He saw no
reason to volunteer information that he had no reason to believe was
known to the Russians. A little while passed—he was still at liberty
—when he was sent for and confronted with the charge that he had
served in the Esthonian Army. From comparative freedom he was
thrown into solitary confinement. He might have lost his reason, he
told me, but for the Shakespeare and Byron he had committed to
memory in his youth. It had been amazing what he was able to draw
from his subconscious mind to distract and console him.

When Emmett told of his arrest in Moscow, the suspicion dawned
on me that it was I who had been responsible for his undoing. I
recounted how the story of his capture had come through while I
was a reporter at the State Department and of how I had seized on it
to accord him a publicity of which I did not envisage the sequel.
"Don't you see?" I said, "There would have been just time for the
newspaper account to get to Russia, three weeks after your capture."

Emmett had so few powers of concentration that he exhibited
little reaction. The next day he headed for the United States. I retain

two images of him: the first, at our meeting in the Hotel Crillon in December 1918, of a boyish figure bubbling over with the joy of life; the second, in Riga three years later, of a flattened-out, pale, and haggard man with all the effervescence gone from him.

A day or two later I met a second protagonist of one of my Washington stories. My report of Colonel Ryan's visit to Russia had made him temporarily one of the most talked-of figures in American public life. When we were introduced I could not resist mentioning my part in a development which had resulted in fateful consequences both for him and me. "So it was you, was it? Well, let me tell you it was no service either to me or the Red Cross."

"You must admit I gave you a lot of publicity."

"To my undoing, yes. Your story hopelessly compromised both the Red Cross and me with the Soviet Government. I had been sent here with the idea of leading a mission to Russia when the moment was ripe. Now the ARA has been chosen and you, the arch villain, are going in with it."

Ryan was a colorful figure who had engaged in medical work in many countries. He died in his prime about 1925 in Persia, where he had been drawn by his adventuresome and restless spirit.

A few days later I crossed the border into Soviet Russia, that grim, strange, fateful new world which presented so striking a contrast to the one I had left behind. I entered it with a receptive mind, bent upon freeing myself as far as possible from all preconceived prejudices. I was as ignorant as most Americans of the historical background of Marxist thought and communism. Social and economic subjects had formed no part of my studies. I had, however, begun to question the essential healthiness of a society which had sent ten million men to slaughter, had been powerless to establish any but an insecure peace, and had made possible in the United States a Harding administration shot through with corruption.

I was curious to discover whether the leaders of Soviet Russia and, in particular, Lenin had anything of a constructive character to offer a world perhaps sick unto death. Wilson had raised a banner to which millions had rallied in their despair. That standard had been dragged in the dust by his own people. Here in Russia an altogether different one had been raised of a more somber and revolutionary nature, terrible in its divisive aspects, remorseless in its brutal aims, reflecting the disenchantment of a people with their former rulers, who had brought one disaster after another upon them.

The first impressions of Moscow were not reassuring. The streets were as unkempt as the people. Most of the stores were boarded up in the absence of private trading. A pall appeared to envelop the city, where the few inhabitants on the streets moved like automatons in a tale of Hoffmann. The impression given was that of a tragic historic pageant. The flight from the ruble reflected the prevailing instability. When we arrived, the dollar commanded a million rubles; a few days later it was five million. No note of a higher denomination than five hundred rubles existed. In consequence, money circulated in packets, the contents of which no one verified. The price of a meal was carried in one's pocket with difficulty.

In all of Moscow but one or two private restaurants remained — for the convenience of foreigners. The population was fed in public kitchens or received a ration for home consumption. I was introduced to a private restaurant, situated in the basement of a building, by Walter Duranty, correspondent of the New York *Times*. The silver and glassware had obviously been assembled from various sources. The clientele was as heterogeneous as the appointments. Guests in threadbare clothing dined alongside a few smartly dressed men and women. It was much as if habitués of New York's Colony and the Bowery had sat down together. Duranty identified the threadbare ones as black marketers who were understandably reluctant to display evidence of their prosperity in the midst of so much misery.

Moscow was filled with foreigners drawn to Russia by the promises of the Revolution. Many were working alongside Russian Communists; the ties of a common political faith transcended those of nationality. In conferences called for the initiation of food shipments to the Volga Basin, I was startled to encounter an Englishman of aristocratic bearing, impeccably dressed, who stood out in striking contrast to his poorly attired Russian associates. Nothing could have been more incongruous in our deliberations with representatives of the Russian working class than his clipped Oxford accent. Personal exchanges were not encouraged and I never learned his identity. He was typical of the extraordinary contrasts which one encountered everywhere at that time in Russia.

The permanent assignment eventually given me was that of assist-

The district supervisor with headquarters at Kazan on the Volga. The district embraced the Tartar Republic and the Chuvash and Mahri oblasts, as well as a number of adjacent regions. It was rich in Russian history and peopled by elements of as diverse culture and blood as were to be found in microcosm in the vast extent of the country: Moslems, Christians, animists, Russians, Tartars, and Bulgars. Heading the operation at Kazan was Ivar Wahren, a naturalized American of an excellent Finnish family, with an adventurous background typical of many in the ARA. He had run away to America, enlisted in the army to learn English, and had risen to the rank of captain.[1]

The food train we were to accompany was finally made up. It comprised a private railway car the government had assigned for our use in Kazan and a sleeping car for a dozen American journalists traveling to report on conditions, Floyd Gibbons in the heyday of his career and Walter Duranty, then on the threshold of success, were among them. As we approached the Volga, where the famine was most dire, dramatic evidence was given of it by hordes of pitiful children with hideously bloated stomachs clamoring for a crust of bread at every station at which we stopped.

Our fellow passengers included one Englishman, Colonel Arthur Lynch, representative of the quixotic individuals drawn to Russia during that period. During the South African War he had become a naturalized Boer and had commanded the Irish Brigade in that conflict against the British. At its close he was tried for high treason and sentenced to death, which was commuted to penal servitude for life. Upon receiving a pardon, he served with the British Army in the First World War and had become a Labor member of Parliament. To the disgust of the Americans aboard, he would leap from the train at every stop to shout, "Long live the Soviets!" It was symptomatic of an ingrained exhibitionism; he had gone through life dramatizing himself by espousing unpopular causes.

Kazan, a city of some 150,000 inhabitants, resembled a center of the dead rather than of the living. All industry had been suspended or radically curtailed for want of raw materials. Retail trade, as in Moscow, was exclusively in the hands of the government, but there was little because of a lack of goods. For living quarters we were assigned a comfortable home formerly the residence of one of the leading merchants. He had been more fortunate than many in that permission had been accorded him to retain the use of the basement.

Georgina Childs, 1922. From a portrait by Nicolai Fechin

J. Rives Childs, 1921. From a portrait by Nicolai Fechin

As we moved in, he emerged from the cellar and was overjoyed to learn we had no intention of evicting him. Private ownership in all homes had been abolished. A few people had been left in occupancy of their former dwellings; some had been permitted the use of one or two rooms; others had been summarily ejected or even executed. The difference in treatment varied with the caprice of the authorities administering the law.

Equally incongruous were the prices for articles of necessity and luxury. Jewelry, precious stones, paintings, and other rare objects commanding fabulous prices abroad went begging as having no practical use. We had been enjoined not to profit from this situation and there were singularly few abuses to my knowledge. Purchase of articles for personal use was not, of course, forbidden. Having need of a fur coat, I bought one from a peddler for $35.00 to discover some months later that the lining, which extended into the sleeves, was of silver fox. I had it removed and made into a jacket for my mother, which a Berlin furrier valued at $1,500. A gentlewoman called one evening and offered for sale a pair of emerald earrings set in diamonds, with a large matching brooch. I knew nothing of precious stones but the earrings pleased me and I bought them for fifteen dollars for my mother. At this same period my future wife was exchanging a sable cape for a pound of butter in Leningrad. Commodities ceased to be quoted in terms of rubles but exclusively in *foonts* of bread. Human existence had been reduced to two great fundamental necessities—food and clothing; nothing else mattered.

Sir Philip Gibbs came to Kazan and we sent him with an interpreter on a day's journey to the Canton of Spassk to observe conditions. Upon his return, deeply shaken by what he had seen, Gibbs was so uncommunicative that it was some time before he could be drawn out. "When we left the ship to go into the interior," he began, "we stopped at the first village. There was not a sign of human activity. We entered a hut and found an entire family huddled on the floor. They had had nothing to eat for days but *lebeda* [a mixture of grass and coarse grain] and were patiently waiting to die. It was the same in all the other huts. Overcome with pity, I offered all the money I had on me, some millions of rubles, to the village headman. He looked at me blankly. 'Comrade, I thank you but this cannot help us. There is no food in the village and no one with sufficient strength to send to the Volga where it might be purchased.' I had thus brought home to me for the first time that money is of value only when it can be converted into a commodity. I could have given these peasants a million pounds sterling but the money would have been of no more use than so many stones." Gibbs later wrote a novel centering on his experiences in Russia, *The Middle of the Road* (1923).

Notwithstanding the famine, the routine of life went on in ways which never ceased to astonish us. There was opera every evening, as well as legitimate theater, to both of which we were given passes. The first night I went to the opera to see a performance of *Carmen* I remarked to a Russian friend I thought it strange the government countenanced theatrical programs when millions were starving a few miles outside Kazan. "Don't judge by appearances," he observed. "There is not a vacant seat here but you may be sure everyone in the audience and even in the cast is suffering from undernourishment, apart from yourself." I was incredulous, but not for long. I went backstage and met Muktarova, a dynamic Persian diva with piercing black eyes and jet-black hair, who sang the title role with great dramatic and vocal power. I invited her and the principal members of the troupe to supper. From the ravenous way they threw themselves on the food I was left in no doubt of the truth of my Russian friend's observation.

Ten years later I became intimate with the Persian Minister to Egypt, Jevad Khan Sineky, who had been Persian consul general in the Caucasus during the First World War. I mentioned one day the unforgettable performance of *Carmen* by a Persian singer, Muktarova, at the height of the famine in Kazan. "Muktarova!" he exclaimed, "it isn't possible. Why, I gave her her start. I heard her singing in the streets of Baku and was so impressed that, when I learned she was Persian, I arranged for her to be given lessons."

My knowledge of Russian was then so inadequate I went only once to the legitimate theater. *Potash and Perlmutter* was being produced, and I thought it might be interesting to see a local production of this American play.[2] When the curtain rose on the first set, one of the opera stars, who had accompanied me, gasped, "My furniture!"

"Was it stolen?" I asked.

She was rippling with laughter. "It was, in a way. When the Revolution broke out, my country home was requisitioned, with everything it contained. You can see some of the pieces on the stage." She shrugged her shoulders. "Why should I complain? I have a well-furnished flat here in Kazan. If my other home is being put to good use, so much the better. *Nichevo*, it doesn't matter." It was a word forever on the lips of Russians and no doubt still is. No expression so perfectly reflects the philosophic resignation of the Slav in the face of every adversity. The Russian has been uttering it during centuries of suffering imposed by one of the harshest climates in the world and under the tyranny of the czars and the terror of the Soviet regime. It is a perfect summation of the attitude of the Russian masses to life.

Theaters were not the only evidence of a cultural flame which remained alive throughout the famine. In late 1921 I attended an exhibit of contemporary painting in a building so insufficiently heated that my teeth were chattering with the cold. The work of one of the artists, Nicolai Fechin, so attracted me I sent for him and proposed he paint my portrait. Delighted with the opportunity to earn something, he fixed the reasonable price of two hundred and fifty million rubles, or fifty dollars. He gave me eighteen sittings, and the result so pleased me that when I was married in 1922 I commissioned him to do my wife's portrait.

While he was making this, I had a letter from an American art lover in Pittsburgh, a Mr. W. S. Stimmel, who had been collecting Fechin's paintings since 1912. He offered to defray his expenses to the United States and to guarantee him work for at least three years if arrangements could be made for his departure. Fechin had received a proposal that he paint the portraits of the Soviet commissars for a Russian Hall of Fame and he was hesitant as to which of the two offers he should accept. In the end he decided to go to the United States and encountered no difficulty in obtaining exit visas from the Soviet authorities for both his wife and himself, while I was able to obtain American visas for them. Once in the United States he found rapid favor. The Chicago Art Institute commissioned him to paint Lillian Gish's portrait for $5,000 and he was soon commanding $10,000 and more for his work.[3]

Shortly after I arrived in Kazan a young man of approximately my age called and, introducing himself as William Simson, stated he was reporting in answer to a request we had made of the local authorities for an interpreter. His thoroughly Nordic features gave him the appearance of a Scandinavian. He spoke impeccable English, had a smart military bearing, and an open, cheerful countenance. I took an immediate liking to him and gave him a desk in my office.

He was to accompany me on every trip I made into the interior. I helped to save his life on one occasion, and a strong attachment was established between us. Even after he had given evidence of possessing superior intelligence, it never occurred to me, in my naïveté, that he had been handpicked by the Soviet authorities to exercise surveillance over our activities and to make sure we were not engaged, under cover of our work, in subverting the existing regime.

As a young man Simson, of Esthonian origin, had been sent to school in London by an Englishman who had taken an interest in him. Of a restless temperament he abandoned his studies to work as a valet at the Savoy Hotel. However friendly we became, he never permitted himself the least familiarity, nor lost the ingrained obsequiousness of a servant. With the outbreak of the Revolution he took a ship at once for Leningrad (then Petrograd), drawn there by much the same urge as that of an insect toward a flame. When the Bolsheviks seized power, he joined the army and, with his innate capacity, rose rapidly in rank.

In one of the periodic purges he was arrested and called up for interrogation in the company of another officer. Simson was the first to be questioned. The examiners were satisfied with his explanations, and he was told he was free to return to his command. What followed I shall give in Simson's words: "I felt seized by some unaccountable impulse which was dictating my behavior independent of my will. At length I spoke up, hardly conscious of what I was saying: 'I came here with that officer,' pointing to my companion, 'and I shall not leave without him.'

"One of my interrogators asked if I were a friend of the other officer. 'I have never laid eyes on him before,' I answered, adding as everyone regarded me incredulously, 'I feel destiny has linked my fate with his and so it will be.'

"The judges shook their heads in bewilderment. The other, when questioned, disclaimed in turn ever having seen me before. They put a few perfunctory questions to him and finally, as if they themselves were being directed by some invisible force, they told us we were both free to go."

Simson moistened his lips. "The sequel will tax your credulity; I tell it as it happened. Some months later I was arrested. The charge this time was a graver one and I thought I was doomed. I was lying in my cell one night, awaiting the end, when the door was abruptly flung open. 'This is it,' I said to myself. Someone came over and, ordering me in a peremptory voice to get up, flashed a lamp in my face. I heard a startled exclamation and a voice, which had lost its harshness, remarked softly, 'It can't be.' I looked up. Bending over me and taking my hand warmly in his was the officer with whom I had linked my fate. He was my judge and might have been my executioner. For all the influence he had acquired, he could not free me unconditionally but arranged for me to be exiled to Kazan. Here I became a translator at the radio station until appointed your interpreter."

However extraordinary the story I did not doubt it. I have more than once felt guided by some invisible hand. Moreover it was typical of those turbulent times. A former czarist general was store-keeper of one of our warehouses; many of our clerical staff were former members of the Russian nobility; the rise and fall of human beings resembled the revolutions of a ferris wheel.

Simson was not the only spy in our midst. There was probably not one of our employees who failed to be called upon for informa-tion about our activities. One of these confided to me she had been summoned by the Cheka and subjected to interrogation. The au-thorities were acquainted with every move I had made; the interro-gation was merely to double-check their information. The papers left in my desk overnight were examined every evening. It was obvious the Soviet Government suspected that, under cover of our relief work, we had other objectives. In the light of our previous armed invasions of Russian territory it was a natural assumption. Our aim, however, was exclusively humanitarian.

There is little recollection today of the notable relief work of the ARA in Russia from 1921 to 1923 notwithstanding that it was one of the most disinterested acts ever undertaken by the United States. Sixty million dollars in food and medical supplies were freely offered a country with which we had no diplomatic representation and which was essentially hostile to us. In contrast to the corruption attending American relief to Nationalist China after the Second World War, there was no graft in our relief work in Russia. In a remarkable resolution adopted by the Council of People's Commis-sars on July 23, 1923, upon the termination of ARA operations, it was stated "the people inhabiting the U.S.S.R. will never forget the help given them by the American people through the ARA." [4]

It was at first contemplated that our aid would be limited exclusively to children, but of what avail to save the children if the parents were left to die? In the end relief was extended to all those in need. By the middle of 1922 we were feeding no less than one million daily in the Kazan district alone, and in the whole of the famine-stricken regions ten million. As we never had more than a dozen Americans in Kazan, we had to rely chiefly on volunteer Russian workers. Wahren and I had been joined by two other Americans, Van Arsdale Turner and John Boyd, as principal executives.[5]

We were not only a very happy family but we were equally fortunate in the Soviet authorities with whom we had to deal. Sabiroff, President of the Autonomous Tartar Republic, of which Kazan was the capital, resembled a lumbering Newfoundland dog. He was painfully conscious of his inadequacies and never pretended to be other than the simple peasant he was. The driving force was Prime Minister Muktarov, an engineer in his early thirties, slim, dynamic, deeply earnest, utterly honest, and entirely consecrated to the Revolution. He was later to lose his life in a Stalinist purge.

The Communists in Kazan and their colleagues in the provinces were generally extremely human, differing but little in their outlook from Americans in comparable walks of life. They were moved for the most part by a single consuming purpose, that of correcting the injustices of the past and of establishing a regime which would remove the causes of war and of human misery. They were persuaded that capitalism had been the root cause of the First World War and that communism would not only bring about universal peace but would introduce a new social and economic Eden.

Except for one initial false start on the part of the authorities in Kazan before we gained their confidence, we never experienced major difficulties in our dealings with them. At the outset of our operations, and with no warning, our office manager and two other Russian employees of the old regime were thrown into prison in flagrant violation of the Riga Agreement granting us freedom in the choice of our personnel. We had been compelled to rely heavily upon men and women of the old regime, who alone possessed a knowledge of English and the abilities we needed. The arrests struck terror in their ranks and threatened the disorganization of our work. As there was no time to consult the Chief of Mission, Colonel William N. Haskell, in Moscow, Wahren and I took counsel together. It was decided to inform Muktarov that unless the arrested employees were released within twenty-four hours all distribution of food would be suspended.

As soon as Muktarov had our ultimatum he sent for us. It was in the evening, the electricity had failed, and we were received in the shadows of flickering oil lamps. His associates, gaunt figures, pinched with hunger, regarded us with ill-concealed hostility. Apart from Muktarov they were largely uneducated, unskilled workers. In their eyes we were members of the capitalist class, their mortal enemies. In view of the coldness of their greeting we speculated as to whether we might not join our three employees in prison before the evening was over.

One of the more fanatical Russians opened the proceedings by denouncing our action in bitter terms. In his view we were prepared to let innocent children starve to protect the skins of three miserable members of the Russian bourgeoisie. We replied the point at issue was respect for an agreement freely entered into by his government. It was late when we left without any conclusive understanding. The next morning, however, our three employees reported at the office. The manager, with terror in his eyes, announced he was resigning. We could do nothing, of course, to retain him against his will.

We were severely taken to task by Colonel Haskell for the draconian character of our action. Yet he was generous enough later to acknowledge that the most successful working relations developed with the Soviet authorities were those in Kazan. Our initial firmness contributed to this in part, but there were also other factors. We avoided assuming any superior airs or a blustering attitude toward men drawn for the most part from humble strata, who would have been the first to take offense at any display of arrogance. We proceeded, moreover, on the assumption they could be trusted. There is no more infallible breeder of misunderstanding than suspicion.

Once we had established the nucleus of an organization in Kazan, our next task was the appointment of committees in the cantonal or provincial centers. Upon these would devolve the responsibility for the organization, within their respective jurisdictions, of county committees, who would in turn set up committees in each village, the whole spreading out fanlike with the main lines of policy under our supervision in Kazan. To ensure a uniform policy and to identify the aid as American, we participated directly in the formation of the cantonal committees. Thereafter, as a further means to those ends, we endeavored through periodic journeys to visit as many county and village committees as possible.

A major problem was transportation. We had only one railway line on which to rely, that connecting Kazan with Moscow and extending only some hundred miles east of us. Our principal lines of transport were the Volga and Kama rivers, on which large steamboats plied except in winter. For our own particular needs the Soviet Government provided us with a steamship. For land transport we relied in summer on carriages or carts and in winter on horse-drawn sleighs. There were regularly established post routes where drivers and horses were available, as throughout Europe in the eighteenth and nineteenth centuries. In winter hundreds of sleighs were mobilized and sent from cantonal centers to take delivery of the food arriving in Kazan by train from Moscow.

In my journeys in the interior I was accompanied by Simson and, until the government gained confidence in us, by Skvartsov, who held the influential post of secretary of the Communist party of the Tartar Republic. He was the keenly intelligent son of a priest, no more than thirty years of age and of inexhaustible energy and a likable, cheerful disposition. I have known few more selfless individuals. He exemplified many Leninist Bolsheviks of those days, with a keen sense of humanity and dedication, with complete disinterestedness, to the ideals of the Revolution. I could not have been more ably seconded in organizing our work outside of Kazan.

On our first journey we headed for Menzelinsk on the Kama River, where we convoked a meeting aboard our steamer to form an ARA committee for that canton. After I had set forth our aims, a teacher, a member of the cooperatives, and a local official were elected. A fanatical Communist denounced the choices on the ground they were not all members of the party. Something of a tumult threatened until Skvartsov intervened. With the authority of his office he announced with finality that the ARA was a humanitarian and not a political undertaking and that the meeting had been properly guided in its selections by objective and not party considerations. A man of Skvartsov's probity was happily spared the purge at Stalin's hands which would otherwise have been his inevitable end. A year later he was transferred to Minsk, where he succumbed to typhus.

Later we were traveling together by sleigh and found ourselves hopelessly lost on the steppes one evening in a violent snowstorm.

No landmarks were visible to our drivers in the great drifts sweeping about us. Alighting from our two sleighs we took counsel of one
another. There was small likelihood we could retrace our steps after
two hours of travel. In remaining where we were we risked being
frozen to death; if we pushed on we might become irretrievably lost
and succumb to exhaustion. I addressed myself to Skvartsov to
inquire his view. For answer he placed his hands akimbo on his waist
and regarded me incredulously. "You ask *me* what to do, you who,
as a foreigner, have come to Russia to aid my people? My dear
friend, it is for *you* to make the decision, not for me."

Despite the peril of our situation I could not avoid smiling at the
vehemence of his outburst. I proposed we push on and trust to luck.
At length, after struggling for half an hour through the mounting
drifts, we espied a faint light ahead. It was the village for which we
had been making. There we sought out the most substantial dwelling
and knocked. A head finally emerged from an upper window.
"Open up and give us shelter," Skvartsov shouted.

"You can't come in here," was the answer. "You must go elsewhere. We have ARA stores and no one is allowed except the
distributors."

Despite our tension and half-frozen state we rocked with laughter.
Upon regaining our composure Skvartsov made known our identi-
ties. The window slammed and in another few minutes we were
being welcomed in the house with deep apologies.

I returned to Kazan convinced the famine was even more disastrous than had been suspected. Unless our aid was stepped up
millions were doomed to die. Moscow began to press us for precise
estimates of our needs. For a close-up survey I volunteered to make
a swing in November through the heart of the famine area.

Three sleighs set out: Simson and I in one (Skvartsov could not
spare the contemplated two weeks' time to make the survey); two
newspapermen, Huddleston and Varges, who had come from Moscow to accompany me, in a second; and rations for our journey in a
third. We never ventured on any trip without our own provisions.
The cold was so intense, at times as low as forty degrees below zero,
that I had equipped myself with fur-lined stockings, felt boots, a
fur-lined hat, my fur coat, and still another coat over the last. Even
with such protection it was impossible to bear the intense cold of an
open sleigh uninterruptedly for more than an hour or two. Nevertheless there was an exhilaration in driving on days of brilliant

sunshine, when there was no wind and the snow was packed hard and firm. At such times the landscape presented a fairylike character. In the eerie silence, broken only by the tinkle of the sleigh bells, one felt all nature was in hibernation.

The thatched peasant huts, ordinarily so drab, presented almost a festive appearance with their festoons of ice and snow resembling Christmas tree ornaments. From the outward appearance of the villages one would never have suspected the tragedy concealed within. The first settlement at which we halted reflected the conditions we found in all. We had stopped for a cup of tea when a group of peasants, who had heard of our arrival, entered the hut. First they turned, as was customary, toward the ikon in a corner of the room and bowed reverently, making the sign of the Cross. A spokesman extended in his hand some *lebeda*, to which the starving population everywhere had been reduced. "Comrades," he said, "we older people may contrive to live a few months on this, but our children must surely die if they are not given other food. Some are already being fed in the American kitchen; cannot all our children be accepted?" There was no note of complaint, no suggestion of a beggar pleading for bread, nor any intimation that the adults were as much in need of food as the children, as was plainly evident.

The most lasting impression of the Russian people gained on these occasions was the simple dignity and heroism with which they faced adversity. In the many famine-stricken villages visited, I was never once solicited for the food we carried for our own needs. In describing their wants they spoke with calm detachment, not as Russians or Communists, but rather as members of the great family of humanity. We drove thousands of miles among a starving population, many facing death, but never once were we molested or our foodstuffs pilfered. Resignation to their fate was their most striking characteristic. In other countries under similar circumstances I would have risked having my throat cut.

We were almost at the end of our journey when Simson began to show signs of exhaustion. A racking headache was followed by violent chills and fever. Fortunately for him we were in a town where a doctor was available. The latter confided to me his fear Simson had contracted typhus; if he were to be saved he had to be rushed to a hospital in Kazan. The nearest railhead was twenty-four hours away by sleigh. I telegraphed, urgently asking that our private railway coach be sent there.

The next morning we set out at four o'clock; we stopped only to change horses and drivers. By evening I was in such a state of fatigue I would throw myself on a bench or the floor of a posting station and fall asleep instantly. The last lap was made in a rough cart driven by a young girl. I was fast asleep on the straw as the cart entered the suburbs of the town at the railhead in the predawn of the second day. Unaccustomed to the bustle of the city, the horses broke into a gallop, the cart was overturned, and I awoke to find my head resting against a brick wall. The fur cap I was wearing had fortunately cushioned the blow.

While we waited for our train, Simson raved in such delirium I wondered whether he would reach Kazan alive. A single precious bottle of cognac remained. I unstoppered it and we quickly finished the quart. Neither Simson nor I received the slightest stimulus, so great was our physical exhaustion and nervous tension after seventeen days of uninterrupted travel by open sleigh in the dead of the Russian winter. During that time we had slept but two nights in beds—on all other occasions we stretched out on the floor of peasant huts.

My report on the conditions I had found persuaded Wahren I should proceed to Moscow to support my account in person. In December 1921 that city presented an entirely different appearance from what it had three months earlier. Store fronts had been unboarded and opened for business by private traders. Hoarded stocks of goods had emerged, as by enchantment, from their hiding places. The faces of people in the streets had taken on new animation, as though awakened from their former torpor. It was as if a magic wand had been waved over the city. This astonishing transformation had been accomplished by Lenin's New Economic Policy, or "Nep" as it was known for short.

Whatever may be said of Lenin, there can be no gainsaying his realism. By a herculean struggle in the years following the Revolution, the Soviet Government had succeeded in overcoming all its enemies but one—nature. The extreme communism into which Russia had been pushed by civil war and the armed intervention of the United States, Great Britain, and France, together with the major famine which had supervened, threatened utter economic prostration of the country. Surveying the situation with his acute perceptiveness, Lenin became convinced that it was a desperate one demanding a desperate remedy. There was one way out—to reverse the engine and introduce a modified form of capitalism. In defending the new policy Lenin announced, with that frankness and humility characteristic of him, "Life has taught us our mistake."

Passing from one improvisation to another in search of a better world, Lenin imparted to the Russian Revolution an epic character. His premature death was a tragedy both for Russia and the world. Born in a family of the lesser nobility at Simbirsk, graduated from the University of Kazan, he was steeped in both Russian and Western culture. There was no trace of vanity in him, nor any self-glorification. A Russian woman of my acquaintance who sought his photograph was asked, "Why do you wish my picture? I am no different from other men."

Two instances may be given of his compassion. One was his plea for clemency on behalf of Rose Kaplan, who had tried to assassinate him in 1918. Another was recounted to me by one of our employees in Kazan, Zena Galitsch, who had been one of Lenin's secretaries. When Béla Kun, serving as military governor of the Crimea after Wrangel's defeat, ordered the execution of ten thousand White officers and sympathizers, Lenin relieved him and summoned him to Moscow. "We had civil peace within our grasp," Lenin told him, "and you, who are not even a Russian, have thrown it away. How can we promote reconciliation with the blood of these victims on our hands?"

In Moscow I made my report and was assured it was being rushed to Washington to further the plans being matured for the extension of our aid. With my task completed, I left in our private car for Kazan. En route I was attacked by violent chills alternating with a burning fever. In Kazan I was put to bed and a local physician was summoned who diagnosed my illness as the dreaded typhus. For five days I was delirious while injections of camphor were administered to strengthen my heart. A special service was held in a Kazan church, where prayers were offered for my recovery. The Associated Press telegraphed the news home, and there were headlines in the Lynchburg press, which made my parents desperate with anxiety. In my delirium I dreamed that Herbert Hoover, then Secretary of Commerce, had cited my report in supporting a request of twenty million dollars from Congress for Russian relief. Six months afterward Christian Herter, then private secretary to Mr. Hoover and later Eisenhower's Secretary of State, visited Kazan. "You will be interested to know," he confided, "that parts of your report were read by Secretary Hoover at a cabinet meeting and helped to spark President Harding's appeal to Congress for funds."

To find distraction in my slow convalescence I began to form a collection of Russian coins. In my boyhood I had collected tobacco tags, cigar bands, and stamps; in my old age it has been books. The task I set myself then was immeasurably facilitated by the presence in Kazan of innumerable sellers with myself as the sole buyer. For guidance I acquired such books as were available on Russian numismatics. These eventually numbered as many as sixty. My collection of coins amounted finally to some 2,600 items, comprising the greatest collection in the world outside the Hermitage Museum. A catalogue I compiled of the copper coins of Peter the Great recorded many that had escaped the attention of Russian numismatists.

When ordered abroad for the completion of my convalescence, I decided to take a substantial number of coins with me and deposit them in Berlin for safekeeping. In the train at Riga I was joined by Walter Duranty and the British High Commissioner to the Baltic. In the company of the latter I hoped to pass unobserved at Eidtkuhnen, the Lithuanian-German border, but these hopes were not realized. The coins were seized. A year later when I returned to Berlin they were delivered to me intact.

III

RUSSIAN QUESTION MARK

I RETURNED to Russia by way of Denmark, Sweden, and Finland. A stopover in Leningrad was to have momentous consequences. On my first visit to the offices of the ARA there my attention was drawn to a strikingly beautiful young Russian girl, with large expressive brown eyes and an air of great distinction. Upon my introduction to her I suggested that we attend the opera together that evening. I had no time for protracted maneuvers since I was obliged to return to Kazan after three or four days, but before I left she had agreed to correspond with me. And that was the beginning of my courtship of my future wife.

Georgina de Brylkine's mother was French, the widow of a Russian naval officer. Both mother and daughter had traveled extensively and were remarkably cultivated. Bent as her mother had been on giving her only child every possible educational advantage, she had placed her in school in Dresden to learn German and at Eastbourne in England to acquire a knowledge of English. A sojourn as paying guest in a distinguished English family in London had been designed to give Georgina some knowledge of the world, while visits to the art galleries of Europe, under her mother's tutelage, had inculcated in her a rare artistic sense.

Mother and daughter had been immobilized in Leningrad by the Revolution. Their story was that of countless members of the Russian nobility. A fortune in securities and jewelry on deposit in a bank had been seized, and they had been left with only such jewels and belongings as were in their personal possession when the Revolution occurred. When their apartment was requisitioned, they had been allowed the use of but two rooms. To gain a ration card, granted only to workers, Georgina found employment in teaching English to Red Army soldiers. As most of these were more in need of instruction in Russian, she was left at length with only three pupils. When she inquired the reason for their continued attendance, she learned they had entered a compact to remain in order that she might continue to receive the Red Army ration card. Although touched by their loyalty, she learned typing to become the secretary of a French businessman, Pierre d'Arcy, an acquaintance of her mother's. When he was imprisoned she was again out of work. She next stumbled upon the home manufacture of woolen shoes when a pair she had made from the threads of a drugget was greatly admired. After she had exhausted, as a source of raw materials, all the carpets in her apartment, the two began selling off their personal possessions for food. They were leading a precarious existence when the ARA opened its doors in Leningrad and Georgina applied for and was given employment.

From Leningrad I returned to Kazan to resume the saving of lives. The battle was a ceaseless one, the transport problem in particular engaging all our ingenuity. Especially was this so in the spring of 1922, when for a period of several weeks, while awaiting the breaking of the icebound rivers, thaws and floods interrupted all distribution of food. The spur track connecting the railway station with the Volga was suddenly washed away over a section of several thousand yards. Until it was repaired, transportation between the river and the station would be at a standstill, and the consequent problem of storing the trainloads of food arriving daily from Moscow would be insoluble.

John Boyd, in charge of shipments, was informed by the Commissar of Transport that the track could not be restored in less than a week. When all his pleas for more rapid action proved unavailing, he went to Karl Schwarz, tough young head of the Cheka. Schwarz telephoned the commissar. "I have Comrade Boyd in my office. You have told him it will take a week to repair the spur track vital for the movement of ARA supplies. I am telling you it must be done in forty-eight hours. It is now 10 A.M. If the track is not completed by noon day after tomorrow, you will be arrested for sabotage. You are aware of the penalty for that."

"We don't have the necessary labor force."

"How many do you need for the job?"

"At least two hundred."

"You will have them in two hours. The rest is up to you. At noon day after tomorrow you will still be the Commissar of Transport or in jail."

Within thirty-six hours the first food train crept over the restored track.

The Cheka, or Ogpu as it was later known, is generally identified abroad as an instrument of political repression. In the early days of the Revolution it had the much broader function of stepping into any economic breech susceptible of shock-troop treatment. It is quite possible that it was through the Cheka that the Revolution survived.

One other example of its effectiveness may be given. I was making an inspection trip by ship on the Kama River from Perm to Chistopol and chose to stop at Izhevsk to inspect our kitchens. When I learned of the presence there of a munitions factory, I suggested to Simson that we visit it. He shook his head. "I wouldn't advise you to seek permission. There is nothing the authorities are more touchy about than defense installations." I accepted his advice without question as I had come to have implicit confidence in him. It was the only instance in which he counseled me against a course of action. He had even encouraged my inspection of prisons, where I had been permitted to chat with political prisoners on the understanding that I would not interrogate them on the reasons for their incarceration.

As Izhevsk I decided to leave the steamer and proceed overland by car to Chistopol, where I would rejoin the ship, but I had not reckoned with the atrocious state of the roads. After exhausting every spare tube and patch, the car limped into a small village on the Kama, where I was fortunate enough to find a telegraph station. I had a pass permitting me to enter any telegraph office in Russia for the exchange of any messages necessary in my work. I seated myself alongside the telegrapher and sent two messages: one to the captain of the ship at Chistopol, directing him to cast off and come for me; the other to the head of the Cheka in Chistopol requesting that he see to the prompt execution of the order. In less than an hour I had a message from the Cheka stating that the steamer had left and would be with me in three hours.

Upon arrival the captain inspected the flimsy wharf and pronounced it quite impractical for the embarkation of my car. His eye caught sight of a pile of lumber which might be made into a temporary platform by his crew. It was suggested that I retire to my cabin and leave the rest to him. The next morning when I awoke we were on our way to the Volga and Kazan, and I needed no assurance that the car was safely aboard. Those were the epic days of the Revolution: there was confusion, there were famine and unprecedented misery, but the machinery of life creaked on under countless extraordinary expedients.

However relentless the ways of the Cheka and the Communist party, there were, at least then, some safeguards against the abuse of authority. On one occasion while traveling with Skvartsov we stopped at a posting station and were informed no horses were immediately available. Using his power as secretary of the Communist party in the Tartar Republic, Skvartsov threatened the head of the local Soviet with arrest unless horses were produced within an hour. The Soviet official scampered off like a frightened chicken to requisition farm horses in the fields. Some months later when I passed through the same village and requested horses, there was such a mad rush to fetch them that Simson and I roared with laughter. I was subsequently called before a judicial authority in Kazan which had the incident under investigation. The head of the village Soviet whom Skvartsov had threatened had brought charges against him for alleged abuse of authority. A series of questions were put to me and my answers taken down in writing. From their tenor it was clear that, notwithstanding the influential post occupied by Skvartsov, he was accountable under the Soviet regime for his official acts.

That summer we had the visit of Colonel Haskell, accompanied by former Governor James P. Goodrich of Indiana, Christian Herter, and a number of others, to inspect our operation. I proposed to Muktarov that the local authorities offer them a dinner, and he readily acceded. As a precaution I telegraphed Wahren, who was traveling with the party, and he confirmed by telegram Haskell's acceptance. Following the arrival of the visitors and a review of our activities, we assembled in the late afternoon at government headquarters for group discussions with the Soviet officials. One of these groups included Haskell, Sabiroff, Simson, and me. Haskell's interrogation of Sabiroff, President of the Tartar Republic, through Simson, as interpreter, went substantially as follows:

Haskell: "How many acres do you expect to harvest this year?"

Sabiroff: "According to preliminary estimates we count on obtaining three-fourths of our needs for the coming year."

Haskell: "I don't believe one word of it."

Although I was unprepared for the lie to be given so brutally to Sabiroff, I had the presence of mind to kick Simson's shins. Taking the hint, he softened Haskell's comment into an expression of doubt.

Sabiroff smiled pleasantly and replied that the government had made a conscientious inquiry, adding in some detail the basis of the estimate.

Haskell: "Tell him he's lying; I came here for facts and not fairy stories."

I administered a second kick to Simson's shins as I gazed incredulously at Haskell. Simson contrived to turn the insult into an innocuous observation, but he could not cover up Haskell's obvious expression of displeasure. For some inexplicable reason Haskell appeared bent on making himself offensive. His most ungracious act was reserved for the end. Arising abruptly from his seat, he remarked curtly: "After listening to this balderdash, it is time to board our steamer."

I reminded him that the authorities, at considerable sacrifice, had prepared an elaborate dinner in his honor which he had accepted; to leave now would be the most signal act of discourtesy he could show them. Even if he did not get away until midnight he would be at Simbirsk, his next stop, by breakfast. With the display of much petulance he finally agreed to stay for one course. I breathed with relief, persuaded that once at table he could be kept for the full dinner. I had reckoned, however, with insufficient knowledge of the intransigent military mind or the capacity of some Americans for discourtesy. Seated next to him at table, I sought vainly to divert him from his declared intention. Upon finishing the soup, he pushed back his chair and invited the other members of his group to take their departure. I have witnessed some extraordinary instances of bad manners but never more studiedly insulting behavior than that of the chief of the Hoover mission to Russia on this occasion to hosts whose dignified demeanor was admirable in the face of such gross conduct. It was fortunate that the excellent relations we in Kazan had built up with the local authorities were in no way affected by the boorishness displayed by our Moscow directors. The test came some months later.

Our little group had become attached to an attractive young Russian girl with whom we skated in winter and played tennis in the summer. Veronica will suffice for her identification, and it need only be said that our group loyalty and respect for her made us treat her as a sister. Then we were joined by an American who failed to share our ideals. Although already married, he looked upon Veronica as legitimate prey. In our indignation at his seduction of Veronica we brought about his recall to Moscow, but the damage had been done; she was unable to forget him.

One afternoon Veronica appeared at our headquarters, as she often did, while John Boyd was in charge. As she kissed him tenderly on the cheek she remarked: "John, you must never forget me." There was a note of poignancy in her voice which startled him. As they chatted, Turner came in from a field trip. With her usual solicitude she followed Turner to his room to relieve him of his impediments. After he had withdrawn to the bathroom to shave, there was the sudden sound of a pistol shot. Investigating the disturbance, Boyd and Turner found Veronica on the floor with a bullet in her brain from the gun Turner had unholstered a few moments before.

When it was evident no earthly aid could restore Veronica to life, John gave orders for a car and chauffeur. "We are going to put her coat and hat on," he said, "and walk her by the guards to the car and take her body home to her parents. That will be the hardest. Then I shall go to Muktarov and seek his cooperation in preventing the Soviet press from seizing on this tragedy to the discredit of the good name we have established in the Tartar Republic. Knowing Muktarov as we do, I think that will be the less difficult task." And so it proved. Muktarov gave his word that not a line would appear in the newspapers and he kept his pledge.

It would be wrong to leave the impression that, in this pre-Stalin period, all Soviet officials were animated by the same good will and integrity as Muktarov. The Muktarovs and Skvartsovs were perhaps exceptional; the tragedy is that, in the absence of American diplomatic representation in Russia from 1918 to 1933, it was not possible to build up their influence. There were, of course, many Communists of quite a different stamp.

In the early summer I returned to Leningrad to pursue my courtship of Georgina. Before my visit ended we went through the civil marriage ceremony required by Soviet law. On appearing before an official for that purpose, we found we needed two witnesses. I appealed to a Red Army sailor and soldier lounging in the corridor, and they readily agreed to sponsor us. After our signatures had been affixed to the wedding certificate, I opened a carton of cigarettes for distribution. The soldier stiffened and explained that he had been happy to act as our witness but he must decline to accept any gift from a member of the bourgeoisie. Two months later I returned to Leningrad for our formal marriage on August 13, 1922, at St. Isaac's Cathedral, Georgina returning with me to Kazan. Georgina had made no inquiry into my financial means, but she excited my hilarity when she asked if we would live in the United States on a scale comparable to that in Kazan. There we had a private railway car and steamer, a car, a chauffeur, and innumerable servants. Twenty-four years elapsed before we even approached that standard.

My collection of coins had been extended to such proportions I had begun to send small packets out of Russia by pouch. Encouraged by the ease with which they passed the frontier, I suggested to my wife's mother that I might send out by the same means some of the treasures she still possessed, including a priceless collection of some sixty eighteenth-century gold snuffboxes. Then I committed two grave errors: the first, in not heeding a warning given me in a dream of the seizure of the collection by the Russian customs; the second, in injudiciously dispatching it in a single packet.

I was in Moscow when news was received that the pouches of the ARA courier had been opened for the first time by Soviet border authorities and the collection of snuffboxes seized, along with certain other contraband belonging to two other members of our mission. There was nothing for me to do but offer my resignation. I was jobless four months after my marriage, but, what was irremediable, my mother-in-law had lost a fortune. It is a tribute to the stoicism of my wife and her mother that neither uttered a word of reproach for this loss.

Happily, my mother-in-law still had possessions of value left. Georgina and I packed up and proceeded to Leningrad to salvage what we could. Paintings by Guardi, Tiepolo, and Repin were taken from their frames and hidden in our baggage. For larger objects which did not lend themselves to concealment, I applied to the Fine Arts Department for an export permit. When a commission of three members, two of whom were of the old regime, called to inspect the property, I readily obtained their approval. It had been ensured by a monetary gratification I had been advised to pass to them in advance. The valuable furniture of the apartment was to be turned over for safekeeping, after my mother-in-law's departure, to the Finnish consulate general. It is probably still awaiting reclamation unless it was destroyed in the bombardment of Leningrad during the Second World War.

I had no difficulty in obtaining an exit visa for my wife as an American citizen but one for her mother presented a more complex problem. It was decided that Georgina and I would proceed to Berlin and there enlist the aid of the German Government in her mother's behalf. The first stage of our journey was to Helsingfors. Aware of the curiosity of Russian customs officials in written instruments, my wife purposely placed a number of letters in full view in each of our bags. As a result, the authorities were so taken up with a minute examination of these that they had no time for anything else.

Once safely past the frontier we glanced at each other with inexpressible relief. Our joy did not spring solely from what was personally at stake. A great weight seemed lifted from us, as if we were emerging from a prison—a reflection of escape from that omnipresent sense of repression bearing down upon everyone in Russia. Yet notwithstanding the atmosphere of terror and the harsh, grim life left behind, I came away convinced that the regime was not only stronger than it was generally credited to be by the outside world but also that there was gestating in the loins of a giant an infant destined to grow in strength. Along with these impressions I recorded also this observation in an article sold to *Current History* but never published:

Five years as head of the Russian Republic has gained for Lenin a hold upon the affections of the Russian people such as no other Communist enjoys or is ever likely to possess. For the great mass of Russians have come to look upon him as the Great Reconciler. When he is dead Russia, no less than the Communist party, will mourn him and with as much if not more reason.

Had Lenin lived and if we had shown more flexibility in our relations with the Russian Revolution, the history of the world might well have taken a different course. With his unerring facility in analyzing the root of a problem, Wilson had declared early in 1917, when Russia dropped prostrate out of the war, that the acid test of Allied war aims would be reflected in Allied treatment of that country. Wilson was singularly ill served, however, by the representative on whom he relied in the subsequent formulation of American policy. The American Ambassador to Russia was David R. Francis, whose rudimentary knowledge of foreign affairs was on a par with that of the political hacks often appointed as American chiefs of mission abroad on the sole basis of financial or other services to a party. The Russian Revolution was outside any terms of reference available to Francis from his experiences as a former governor of Missouri. He interpreted one of the great historic events of the modern world as comparable to a Central American revolution which would splutter and die or might be repressed by force of arms. Viewing it thus, he abandoned Leningrad for Vologda for greater security, refusing all overtures from Lenin and Trotsky for the continuance of relations on even an informal basis.

Nor was this the only error of judgment. We thought that if we moved troops into Russia, law and order would be restored and life would return to normal, as it inevitably did in Latin America after each American intervention. Once American political democracy had been introduced by American bayonets and free elections proffered to a people unacquainted with them, Americans might sleep peacefully in their beds. So it was that Wilson was influenced to order American troops into Russia in Siberia and at Archangel. Their ostensible purpose was to protect American war supplies and to cover the "retreat" of Czechoslovakian forces.

Other Americans of standing in Russia had a much firmer grasp of the realities of the situation than did Francis. Raymond Robbins, of the Red Cross, General William S. Graves, commanding American forces in Siberia, and an obscure foreign service officer, Felix Cole, had a far clearer appreciation of the historical forces at work. Writing to Washington on June 1, 1918, from the American consulate at Archangel, Cole made a realistic appraisal:

The Socialist Revolutionaries, Mensheviks, and Cadets who now advocate intervention are discredited officeholders seeking to regain power. . . . The very men who now pray for our bayonets are the ones who did more than even the Bolsheviks to ruin the Russian front. The men who do rule Russia, however badly it is done, are the small [group of] Bolshevik leaders.[1]

If the consequences of our misguided Russian policy in 1917 and 1918 were of enormous significance to us, they were even more fateful to the Russian people. The greatest single factor in welding the Russian people together and in strengthening the Soviet regime was Allied armed intervention. It had, moreover, another hardly less momentous result: it pushed the Bolsheviks into measures which came to be known as "war communism" and thus definitely and directly contributed to the rigidity and extremism of the regime. Perhaps the greatest mistake arising out of armed intervention was our want of success. We should either have assigned sufficient forces to have ensured the overthrow of the Soviet Government or we should have effected some accommodation with the Bolsheviks. We did neither, with the result that our intervention not only strengthened the government but sowed a suspicion and distrust of us which have never been eradicated.

No nation can break precipitately the bonds of its historic past. The democratic institutions we have found suitable for our own needs are a development of centuries. That they suit us is no assurance they will have some magic property for Russia, China, Indonesia, or Africa.

Although I left Russia in 1923 with a sense of relief at escaping a repressive atmosphere alien to an American but quite natural to a Russian, I left also with deep admiration for the sincerity of such Communists as Muktarov and Skvartsov in their endeavors to make a new world out of the dying embers of the old.

IV

PALESTINE PROBLEM AND RUMANIAN OPERETTA

O**N LEAVING** Russia I was confronted by the necessity of determining my future career. My choice was to return to journalism. On the strength of a series of articles on Russia contributed to the *Christian Science Monitor* after returning home, I was offered a post as that newspaper's correspondent in Russia, independent of the representative already there. But the life of a newspaperman was too bohemian an existence for my wife; the consular service appealed to her much more. That settled it. In the summer of 1923 I studied for the examinations. The written test presented no particular difficulties; it was the oral which was decisive. Applicants were received in groups of five by a board of examiners which included Wilbur J. Carr, chief of the Consular Bureau, and Leland Harrison, Assistant Secretary of State. As the only candidate in the group applying for appointment as full consul I was subject to a particularly searching scrutiny. In quick succession I was asked by Harrison to define the character of each of the three classes of mandate territories of the League of Nations. My answers were perhaps a little too glib to suit him. His next question was obviously designed to baffle me—that I define the purposes of the International Communications Conference of 1921. I answered as if I had been present at the conference sessions. In a way I had been, having reported the initial stages for the Associated Press. Happily for me Harrison was unaware of this. Finally, he asked what disposition had been made at the conference of the island of Yap. He had me there and it was probably just as well. I had been in Russia, beyond the reach of newspapers, when the decision as to Yap had been made, and I proffered this as an excuse for my ignorance. Some little while later I received an official communication from the State Department informing me that I had passed, having been one of a dozen approved out of approximately a hundred candidates. In October I was called to Washington for a brief course of instruction before being sent to the field.

It was only much later that I was able to appreciate how appallingly inadequate was the guidance given us. No least intimation was forthcoming that we should measure our words, interpreted as they would be by foreigners as expressive of the viewpoint of the government we represented. It was years before I realized, what should have been emphasized then, that a foreign service officer ceases to have the privilege of expressing his own mind until his retirement. Nor were we instructed about those accepted conventions of official and social relations traditional with diplomacy. It may have been due to that anomaly in the American character which makes a fetish of etiquette books and yet is amused by the practice of etiquette on the part of diplomats under the name of protocol. In short, we were sent out to sink or swim, and it is a small wonder that some of us sank beneath the surface in the process, myself among them.

My first assignment was as consul to Jerusalem, where I was subordinate to an older officer of the same grade as I. My income had suffered a substantial decline from that enjoyed at the Peace Conference and with the ARA. During these years I was troubled by a continually recurring dream in which I saw myself entering the Associated Press bureau in Washington to apply for my old position, the result, no doubt, of a subconscious feeling that I had made a false move in abandoning newspaper work for the foreign service. What kept me from chucking in my hand during the eighteen years of virtual stagnation which extended from 1923 to 1941 was a sense of pride, a determination to gain the recognition I felt would be mine in the end.

In 1923 there were few more interesting countries in the world than Palestine. When we arrived it was still Arcadian in its simplicity and peacefulness. Two thousand years had elapsed since the Jews had ruled over any part of it. Arabs comprised 90 per cent of the population, the Jews less than 10 per cent. If any country warranted preservation of its age-old aspect, reflecting as it did so many biblical ways, it was Palestine. The First World War and Hitler decisively transformed it.

The first seeds of the Palestine problem were sowed in 1917 by the Balfour Declaration, a British wartime measure to rally Jewish support for the Allied cause. There was no mention in the Declaration of a Jewish state; all it contemplated was the establishment "in Palestine of a national home for the Jewish people." It contained an important limiting provision, of which less and less was to be heard thereafter, namely, that in the attainment of the Declaration's objective "nothing shall be done which may prejudice the civil and religious rights of existing non-Jewish communities in Palestine." These two provisions were soon found to be mutually irreconcilable in practice. Implicit in the first was Jewish immigration into Palestine. Yet this was unrealizable on any scale without prejudice to the rights of the preponderant Arab population.

From the establishment of the British mandate in 1922 until its relinquishment in 1948, British policy oscillated between emphasis on one or the other of these two incompatible aims, depending upon the shifting international situation and, in particular, on the degree of pressure brought to bear on the sorely tried British by the American Government, acting in response to the clamor of American Zionists. As any measure of self-government was obviously precluded, since the first act of an Arab majority would have been to check Jewish immigration, Palestine was administered by the Colonial Office through a British High Commissioner.

The first to occupy that office was a distinguished British Jew, Sir Herbert Samuel. The impartial discharge of his impossible task quickly earned him the respect of Arabs and Jews alike, apart from the extreme Zionist wing bent on the establishment of a Jewish state. That objective, however, was for long kept sedulously in the background.

Seconding Sir Herbert Samuel was an exceptionally able group of officials. They included Sir Gilbert Clayton, Sir Ronald Storrs, and Sir Norman Bentwich. I have met few more gregarious Englishmen than Storrs, governor of Jerusalem. There mingled together in his home on Sunday afternoons a colorful variety of representatives of the many different races and religions in Jerusalem: Arabs, Jews, and Christians, including Armenian, Coptic, Roman Catholic, Greek Orthodox, and Protestant religious dignitaries. Whatever their clashing beliefs and purposes, they found common ground in the home of Pontius Pilate's successor. Today such gatherings would be unrealizable.

There was one outstanding figure in Palestine, ardent in the advocacy of a program which offered promise of a durable Arab-Jewish understanding. This was Dr. Judah Magnes, both a great Jew and a great humanitarian, head of the Hebrew University. His countenance was radiant with benevolence and he was Christlike in his dealings with his fellowmen. He was even then espousing, and continued to champion until his death in 1948, a binational state, based on a genuine Arabian-Jewish partnership. Had his wise counsel prevailed there would be peace today in Palestine and concord between Jews and the Arab world. William Zukerman, an American, wrote of him in the *Jewish Newsletter* of April 21, 1958: "He was both a moral leader and a seer who predicted with remarkable clarity the grave dangers into which militant nationalism would lead Jewish Palestine and the Jewish people."

Of many notable figures who had been attracted to Palestine with whom we became closely acquainted, the most distinguished American was Edward Blatchford from Chicago, head of the local Y.M.C.A. He was one of those incurable idealists who entertain the quaint notion that man is a reasonable animal, who may be argued into decent behavior. The passion then germinating between Zionists and Arabs in Palestine should have given him pause and caused him to question how far men may be influenced by persuasion. An Olympian few such as Judah Magnes were open to reason, but the tragedy of Palestine was that neither then nor afterward were men of his vision shaping events.

Blatchford once asked me to make one of the addresses at a "Golden Rule" luncheon he was organizing to promote greater understanding between members of the diverse faiths and communities in the country. I accepted when he assured me that the principal officer of the consulate had declined to be present and would not take it amiss that I speak for the American community. I went about the preparation of my address with great care. For my introductory text I took a quotation from Woodrow Wilson: "Do you covet honor? You will never gain it by serving yourself. Do you covet distinction? You will gain it only as the servant of mankind." Mindful that the audience would include many Moslems and British, I offered as examples the nobility of Saladin toward his Christian foes and that of Wilberforce in his campaign against slavery. Almost everyone of any prominence was at the luncheon. I was the last to be called on and, as I rose, I observed the mild surprise on the part of those present. To most of them I was unknown. My address was so well received that my wife and I were thereafter showered with invitations.

When Sir Herbert Asquith, former Prime Minister, was the guest of the Storrs, we were invited to an intimate dinner of ten to meet him. Asquith had just come from Cairo, where he had been visiting General Edmund Allenby, British High Commissioner, when Sir Lee Stack had been murdered by Egyptian nationalists and Allenby had addressed to the Egyptian Government one of the stiffest ultimatums ever delivered by the British Government. According to Asquith, he had declined Allenby's invitation to participate in its drafting on the ground that he was not a member of the government.

Living in Palestine was like having one's residence in a museum, and there was no better guidebook to it than the Bible. Not all biblical sites commanded equal reverence, and in this respect the Church of the Holy Sepulchre in Jerusalem was sadly compromised. Within its sacred precincts there were not infrequent hand-to-hand encounters between priests of different faiths over some alleged trespass upon the specific areas allotted to each. So intense was the bitterness of this rivalry that the keys of the church had long been in the keeping of a Moslem. A Christian could not be trusted with the custody of Christ's reputed tomb! As if the burial place were insufficient to excite the awe of pilgrims, a mark on a flagstone within the church was exhibited as Adam's footprint and an aperture in a rock was pointed out as the original resting place of the cross.

Nothing, however, could so strain credulity as the annual ceremony of the Holy Fire. On Greek Easter Friday in 1924 I witnessed it at firsthand amid thousands of the devout—and a few who had been drawn by curiosity, as had I. As we watched, Greek Orthodox priests filed into the covered crypt in the church's center. At precisely eleven a powerful flame burst through a flue extending horizontally from the tomb. The worshipers pressed to ignite their candles from a fire they looked upon as a miraculous emanation from God, with apparently no least suspicion that it might have been lit by the priests. So great was the crowd's excitement that British soldiers were obliged to crack long whips over the heads of the multitude in the church to prevent the fatalities which had often resulted theretofore. It was sad testimony of man's gullibility.

After a few months in Jerusalem a sense of callousness toward many of the outward symbols of religion was a not uncommon development. At the consulate, when we received requests from the United States for Jordan water for baptismal purposes, we would fill a phial from the tap instead of troubling to obtain it from the river. It was not only more convenient for us but, in our irreverent view, the recipient would be no worse for being baptized by Palestinian water of other than Jordan origin.

One of the great charms of life in and about the Near East, where I was destined to spend my entire diplomatic career, was the interlocking character of links formed in one country with those in others. Contributing to this was the Moslem faith common to Near Eastern countries generally and the part personal relations played in them all.

Probably no American between the two World Wars exercised a greater influence in that area than Charles R. Crane, an American industrialist and public-spirited citizen, at one time American Minister to China. His first contact with the Moslem world occurred in 1918, when he was sent to Palestine at the instance of President Wilson and the Peace Conference as a member of the King-Crane mission. After investigation the mission reported that if the principle of self-determination was to be taken into account and "the wishes of Palestine's population to be decisive it would be necessary to limit Jewish immigration and to abandon any plan to make Palestine a Jewish State." [1]

Crane's visit awakened his interest in the Arab world, with the result that in the early 1920's he sent an American engineer, Karl Twitchell, to Yemen and Saudi Arabia with an offer of technical assistance to be paid for by Crane with no *quid pro quo* asked in exchange. So impressed was King Ibn Saud by this initial American contact and such was the favor gained by Twitchell with the Saudi Arabian monarch that when American oil interests sought concessions, which subsequently were developed by the Arabian American Oil Company, they found it advantageous to use Twitchell as an intermediary. Thus Crane, who never derived any financial profit from American oil concessions, was the sire in great part of that American network spreading about the Persian Gulf.

Later he conceived the idea of subsidizing a group of young men to follow the revolutionary ideas brewing in China, Russia, and the Near East. For the last-named area Crane's choice fell upon George Antonius. George was a Christian Arab from the Lebanon who, after graduation from Cambridge, had entered the British Colonial Service and had been posted to Palestine in the Educational Department. He later left it and through the generosity of Crane was enabled to devote himself exclusively to research and study. I still retain a keen memory of how captivated my wife and I were when we first met George in 1924 at a reception given by Sir Herbert Samuel for General Maxime Weygand, French High Commissioner for Syria and Lebanon, at Government House. It developed into one of the closest relationships I was to form in the Near East, a friendship terminated only by George's untimely death during the Second World War. This loss the Near East could ill afford as there were few men better qualified than he to interpret to the West Arab purposes and aspirations.

Shortly after our meeting and the rapid flowering of our friendship, George and I, accompanied by my wife, hired a car to make one of the first tours by motor of the archaeological treasures of Jordan at Amman, Madeba, Mishetta, and Kerak. At Amman, in the absence of Emir Abdullah, we were received by his uncle, Emir Shaker, who had been tapped for immortality in T. E. Lawrence's *The Seven Pillars of Wisdom* (1926). At a dinner in tents erected on hills overlooking ancient Philadelphia, we had our first taste of Bedouin hospitality. The principal dish was a whole sheep. As a special mark of favor Emir Shaker plucked one of the eyes from it with his fingers and offered it to my wife. She, in no way disconcerted, slipped it unconcernedly into her mouth, as if sheep's eyes were a staple of her diet.

Present was a handsome fair-haired young Arab, Emir Adel Arslan, of a princely Druse family, who had been made a member of the Jordanian cabinet after his expulsion from Syria by the French. It seemed singular to me at the time that a Syrian should be accorded a government post in another country, but it was in no way unusual, as I was to find later in Saudi Arabia and Yemen. The desert Arab is as untouched by a sense of nationality as the European was in a similar feudal stage of development. The Moslem faith is the binding tie as Christianity was in the Europe of the Middle Ages.

Arslan was our guide to Jerash, a Greco-Roman city in the vicinity of Amman which, along with ancient Philadelphia, offered impressive testimony to the once vast extent of Rome's political power. Britain and France had recently come upon the scene, but their rule was to be even more transitory than that of Rome. "Asia is a very tempting morsel," the French diplomat and philosopher, Comte de Gobineau, once wrote, "but one which poisons those who feed upon it."

I was to meet Arslan again, in Egypt in 1931, in Baghdad in 1934, and in Istanbul in 1949, where I found him Syrian Minister to Turkey. Both he and George Antonius immeasurably furthered my way in the Moslem world. Through George I was to be introduced in 1931 to the newspaper circles of Cairo, then largely controlled by Lebanese and dominated by his father-in-law, Dr. Faris Nimr, editor of *Mokattam*. Through George and Arslan I formed a warm friendship with an obscure Egyptian journalist, Abdul Rahman el Azzam, who subsequently became an important official of the Arab League and who was instrumental in obtaining for me a favorable entree in Riyadh years later. Finally, these interlocking threads brought me in contact with Charles R. Crane in Cairo, where he came every winter and where I first met him in 1931, and with Karl Twitchell, whose path crossed mine again in Saudi Arabia a quarter of a century after our first encounter. Crane twice presented me with books which were to have a direct relationship to my work in two other countries of the Near East: Iran and Saudi Arabia. It was a time in the 1930's when George Antonius was devoting himself to the study of the Arab nationalist movement which found fruition in *The Arab Awakening* (1939), a classic study of the subject.

I was at my first post in Jerusalem only a little more than a year. A crisis arose in my relations with my chief. Bewildered as a bird in a cage I saw only one solution, to decline to serve under him until an inspector was sent from Washington to investigate our differences. I thus committed the unpardonable sin of not getting along with my superior officer. As a result I was sent to "Coventry," namely to the consulate general at Bucharest, Rumania, where I would be passed over for promotion for four years.

When I went to Jerusalem in 1923, I had been imbued with high hopes regarding a new career in the foreign service; I went to Bucharest thoroughly disillusioned. What tempered my depression was to find in Bucharest Eliot Palmer, later Ambassador to Afghanistan, a chief of high competence and understanding who, with his exceptional wife, Eno, became our lifelong friends. But for them I might have given up. One of Eliot's passions was the furtherance of the careers of his subordinate personnel. His attitude toward members of the public who appealed to the consulate general for service was equally positive. "Don't examine the regulations to find an excuse for refusing a request but rather for a reason to grant it," was his guiding principle.

We could not have been a happier official family. In addition to

Palmer and myself, there were two officers junior to me: George Arnold and John H. E. MacAndrews. The latter, with his Irish blarney, was the most popular American in the city. It was perhaps his wit that had endeared him to King George of Greece, then living in exile. Mac and his sister Kate, dependent on his small salary for their living, had a walk-up, third-floor apartment. For all its inconvenience, from time to time they entertained the royal couple at dinner. For such parties they would save up over an extended period, employ a servant for a few weeks, and, after discharging their accumulated social obligations, dismiss her and resume a life of severe economy.

With my small income my wife and I were but little better off. The only quarters we could find within our means were four rooms in the attic of a Rumanian banker, to which our only access was by the servants' entrance. We would have been wiser to have chosen a less fashionable district; we would have done so if it had been consonant with my official position. Not one of us at the consulate, including the consul general himself, could afford a motor car or membership in the local country club.

Under such circumstances my wife and I were able to extend our social contacts but slowly. Eventually our friendships grew to include not only Americans, with a few French and British, but a widening circle of Rumanians. In this we were markedly different from most Americans and British. With that strange insular attitude characteristic of many Anglo-Saxons abroad they regarded most Rumanians disdainfully as "natives."

From the outset of my foreign service career I had considered it incumbent on me to form close relations with the people of the country in which I might be stationed. My wife, with her cosmopolitan outlook, fully shared my view that this was an obligation forming part of our official duties. At that time it was not common to many American and British diplomats, who moved for the most part in a goldfish world. In October 1934 and in April 1935 I voiced the opinion in the *American Foreign Service Journal* that the smart society to which diplomatic officers largely restricted themselves had ceased to be representative and that it behooved us to acquaint ourselves with less conventional circles if we were to gain awareness of the new forces everywhere at work. My views were so unorthodox that the editor commented cautiously that, although they opened up "a fruitful field of discussion," there were "many officers

American Minister Bert Fish emerging from Abdin Palace, Cairo, after presenting his letter of credence to King Fuad in 1933

Triumphal procession relief, Achaemenian Palace, Persepolis. (Courtesy of the Oriental Institute of the University of Chicago)

who do not share them." It is a mark of the gulf that separates us from that era that today an officer in dissent would be judged wanting in the proper fulfillment of his duties.

I had been charged with the economic work of the consulate. It was a particularly challenging assignment because I had never pursued the study of economics or the social sciences. To equip myself I had to rely on self-instruction, and for that I needed books, but I lacked the funds to pay for them. In my extremity I seized the opportunity offered by the *Christian Science Monitor* to become their Rumanian correspondent. It was contrary to the regulations, but it was the only way available to me short of robbing a bank to fulfill adequately my new duties. As a cover I arranged that one of the Rumanian employees receive the nominal appointment and under his name the news reports went out. With this addition of about forty dollars monthly to my income I sent for the syllabus of the London School of Economics and from it made choice of the books which I considered essential for acquiring the economic background of which I was in need. In addition to economic theory and practice, I extended my reading to a number of classic works in the social sciences. These opened a new world to me.[2]

It was not long before the consulate general at Bucharest became one of the first half dozen offices in the service in the number of its economic reports graded excellent. Some months later I was both gratified and amused to receive a letter from Wallace Murray, chief of the Division of Near Eastern Affairs, in which he informed me of "the great prestige" which I had gained in the Department of State by my economico-political reports, which he was generous enough to term "remarkable." At the same time he inquired where I had gained my knowledge of economics. I was obliged to tell him that I had never had a formal course on the subject from professors.

My five years in Bucharest from 1925 to 1930 coincided with the period of mad speculation culminating in the Wall Street crash of October 1929. The economic unhealthiness of that era was evident in Rumania no less than in the United States. Banks were paying 15 to 18 per cent on time deposits, and loans were being made at a minimum interest rate of 30 per cent, extending to as high as 40 per cent. Yet notwithstanding this economic storm warning, American bankers stood in the waiting rooms of the Rumanian Minister of Finance and of local banks pressing upon them loans of excess American capital which investors were bent on placing abroad. Ivar

Kreuger, with loans from the United States, came to Bucharest at this time to acquire the Rumanian match monopoly against the payment of millions, which were shortly to vanish. The representative of at least one American banking syndicate remained for more than a year, endeavoring to persuade the Rumanians to take advantage of the substantial loan he was prepared to make them. It was a strange inversion of roles between debtor and creditor. The looming disaster, could not have been more pointedly prefigured than in a conversation in which I participated about 1928 between a visiting American banker, Brown, and the Rumanian president of a local bank, Ionel Protopopescu, who, with his wife, had become our closest Rumanian friends. Here in substance are the views they exchanged.

P: Speculation on the New York Stock Exchange and the economic policies of your government have an ominous aspect to me. There are three means available to Europe to discharge its debts to the United States: one, through our exports, which you refuse to accept because of your tariff policy; two, with gold, which we do not have; and, three, through services and other invisible exports which are limited in character for us.

B: You have forgotten the factories in Europe, ownership in which may be transferred to the United States as payment of Europe's obligations.

P: And the income from these?

B: It may be reinvested in Europe.

P: With the result that Europe will eventually become the economic vassal of America. What will happen to the Europeans?

B: That is simple; they will receive wages and salaries from their American entrepreneurs.

P: Thank you. . . . You will excuse me if I say your solution smacks of Alice-in-Wonderland economics.

B: It is not original with me; it represents the thinking of our most conservative bankers. Forget about the principles of classical economy. They cannot account for the boom on the New York Stock Exchange. We are developing new principles of economy.

P: I hear an ominous echo of the past. Remember John Law and the Mississippi Bubble?

B: Our boom is unprecedented; it is ushering in a period of perpetual prosperity.

P: We have heard such a siren call, luring investors to their ruin, over the centuries.

B: My dear Sir, ten, twenty years hence I hope to meet you again here. You will then recall our conversation and have to acknowledge that I was right.

Poor Brown never returned to Rumania. He may have been one of those who jumped out of a window in Wall Street the following year. If he had returned to Rumania, he would not have found Protopopescu; he had died after the failure of his bank consequent upon the closing of the doors of the Credit Anstalt in Vienna, which had been the slight gust of wind precipitating the overthrow of the financial structure of Europe built on American sand. If he had returned in 1948, he would have found Nina Protopopescu, once one of the most elegantly dressed women in Bucharest, living in a small room with six other persons in what has become known as the People's Democratic Republic of Rumania. It is perhaps too much to suppose that if Brown is still alive, he would agree that the folly of our political and economic policies in the post-Wilsonian era may have contributed appreciably to Europe's collapse.

In 1930 I was dining with a number of prominent financial figures in the New York home of Percival Farquar, an international promoter. As we emerged from dinner our eyes caught the headline of an evening newspaper: HOOVER SIGNS SMOOT-HAWLEY TARIFF. Although the guests were staunch Republicans, there was not one present who did not deplore the approval by the President of the highest tariff wall ever erected by the United States, foreseeing as they did the disruptive effect it would have on European economy. It was one of the last acts of madness of that "unprecedented and perpetual period of prosperity." Only a short time later Hoover had to declare a moratorium on the collection of European debts to America. My mind went back to Lenin and Russia. Was it indeed true, as Lenin and Marx had contended, that capitalism bore within itself the seeds of its own destruction?

Early in 1930, while preparing the annual review of commerce and industries for 1929, the conviction began to grow on me that Rumanian economy was likely to be severely threatened if the Soviet Five-Year Plan fulfilled even a part of the expectations formed of it. Some 90 per cent of Rumania's exports were lumber, livestock, wheat, and oil, which were already being seriously undercut by Russia in Rumania's traditional Near Eastern markets. In the general review submitted to the Department of State of May 17, 1930, I wrote:

With the conspicuous identity which exists between the export trade of Rumania and the growing volume of Russian exports of cereals, oil products and lumber from neighboring Black Sea ports, the future of Rumanian economic development is inevitably bound up with Russian economic development. Continued expansion of Russian exports of commodities upon which the Rumanian trade balance is so completely dependent may have far-reaching consequences in the distinguishment of which no prophetic insight is needed.

Barely four months elapsed before Virgile Madgearu, Rumanian Minister of Commerce, appeared before a commission of the League of Nations Assembly in Geneva on September 22, 1930, to plead for a preferential European tariff for Rumanian products as "a matter of life and death." In support of his request he pointed out that, as a result of the reemergence of Russia in world markets, Rumanian exports had declined in 1929 by 20 per cent. The country was being threatened with economic disaster.

I was beginning to suspect that the economic squeeze might extend to a political one. On returning to the United States in 1930, I observed aboard our ship Leahu, Rumanian consul to Chicago and nephew of Prime Minister Jules Maniu, studying German. "Better start studying Russian," I laughingly suggested. "The future fortunes of Rumania are more likely to be linked with Russia than Germany. Germany is far away, Russia is next door." He looked at me incredulously as if I were pulling his leg. The truth was we were all living in a fool's paradise, some a little more so than others.

Occasionally I went to Vienna as courier for the American Legation. I had read in the *Manchester Guardian Weekly* of the workers' flats which the Socialist municipality of Vienna had built after the First World War. The idea of constructing homes for workers anywhere outside Soviet Russia was so revolutionary that I was curious to visit them. I seized the occasion of my next trip to Vienna to do so. I was so impressed by what I saw, including the nurseries to care for children while the parents were working, that upon my return I conveyed an expression of my interest in what had been accomplished to the Austrian Minister in Bucharest.

In my naïveté I had not anticipated his reaction. "It's nothing but

Bolshevism," was his comment. "We taxpayers are being bled white by those radicals who are running Vienna."

My own opinion was that it was good insurance against the possibility of violent revolution in the future, but it was not for me to argue the point. What I thought should be of concern was how the revolutionary forces which were brewing could be controlled.

In Rumania the signs of social disintegration were widespread; the ruling class seemed intent on digging its own grave. There was probably no more corrupt country in Europe. A so-called parliamentary government was in reality a veiled dictatorship. The King would dissolve parliament at the behest of a faction and invite a new Prime Minister to form a government. The one so named invariably obtained a majority in the elections conducted under his auspices. In 1926 General Alexandru Averescu, with but a handful of deputies in his party, was named Prime Minister in this game of musical chairs and had no difficulty in gaining a majority in the ensuing elections. A year later when he was displaced not a single deputy of his party was returned; his successor had seen to that.

Corruption in the Ministries was such that bribery was taken for granted. An American who submitted a bid for mechanical saws was outraged when the contract was let to a German competitor whose price was substantially higher. When he protested he was blandly informed that the higher the price the greater the rake-off to those who were letting the contract; he should have known this and acted accordingly.

Even the royal family was not exempt. When Queen Marie visited the United States her lady-in-waiting, Mme Simonne Lahovary, informed one of the leading department stores in New York that Her Majesty was interested in visiting it but would expect a contribution of $5,000 to her charities. In expressing his gratification the manager observed that as the concern was governed by a board of directors he would have to obtain specific authorization to make the contribution requested. Would Mme Lahovary be so good, therefore, as to send him a letter on the subject which he would be happy to submit to his board? He was pleasantly surprised to be informed that the letter would be received without delay.

When the letter was in his hands, he promptly telephoned Mme Lahovary that all arrangements were being made to receive Her Majesty with appropriate ceremony on the date she had proposed.

"And the check for Her Majesty's charities?"

"Unfortunately the board has not found it possible to approve such a disbursement."

"In that case, of course, Her Majesty will be unable to come."

"I suspect she will," the manager purred, "or else it will be impossible for us to withhold the letter from the local press."

If our five years in Rumania were difficult ones owing to our stringent financial circumstances, they were not without other compensations. Although lacking a car, we were frequently invited by the Protopopescus and Baron Henri de Malval, a Frenchman with whom a life friendship was formed, to accompany them on extended excursions. It was thus that we explored the extraordinarily varied regions making up Rumania, including Transylvania, where German colonists had been settled in the Middle Ages to form Christendom's barrier against the Turks, as well as Bukovina and the Dobruja, all with their mosaics of peoples. Gypsies everywhere added song and color to a delightful country. The scene suggested that of an operetta in which colorfully dressed peasants, in costumes which were indicative of their particular village, moved in endless procession across the stage.

Settled by soldiers of Trajan, the country was a mixture of Slavs, Latins, Germans, Hungarians, Bulgarians, Turks, Greeks, and gypsies. The language was a compound of Latin, Slavic, Turkish, and Greek; its culture bore a strong Byzantine stamp. With its fertile wheat fields, the deep forests of the Transylvanian Alps, and its savage grandeur peculiarly suited to be the background of so macabre a tale as *Dracula*, Rumania was an entrancing country.

V

BY THE BANKS OF THE NILE

MY ECONOMIC and political reports were presumably responsible for my nomination early in 1930 as second secretary and consul in Cairo. I was to assume charge of the consulate and serve at the American Legation as circumstances might warrant. Although the diplomatic and consular services had been amalgamated in 1924, there had not yet been that physical fusion subsequently effected.

Before I left Bucharest, an Englishman offered me this counsel: "You have made a point of mixing with Rumanians, but you will find it impossible to consort socially with Egyptians. No one does, and if you should persist you will be ostracized by the British and American communities." I remarked that if I were to learn anything of Egypt it was more important that I get to know the people of that country than the British and American colonies; if in the process I excited the disfavor of foreign residents, I was prepared to run that risk. Aboard ship between New York and Alexandria an American married to an Englishman in the Sudan gave me further advice: "The English will first endeavor to freeze you out. When they find they can't, they will take you in." Her counsel proved more useful than that given me in Bucharest.

We arrived in Egypt late that year. George Wadsworth, first secretary of the legation, put us up until we found an apartment in Garden City. I would have been unable to support the financial burden of a diplomatic secretary had the government not begun in 1930 to bear the cost of living quarters abroad for its officers. I was no longer obliged to live in an attic but could choose a flat in keeping with my official position.

I had been at the consulate only a few days when I was summoned to the legation by the minister, William N. Jardine. He had been president of Kansas Agricultural and Mechanical College and, as an authority on farming, had served as Coolidge's Secretary of Agriculture. Jardine was a breezy midwesterner who had been totally unacquainted with diplomacy when he assumed, a few weeks earlier, his new duties as American Minister to Egypt. Frank to admit his diplomatic incapacity, Jardine had entrusted to Wadsworth's hands technical direction of the legation.

Jardine now confided to me that personal differences had arisen which made Wadsworth's transfer desirable. As the only other secretary immediately available I would have to step into the breach. Did I have sufficient confidence to assume a work of which he himself knew nothing? Consular affairs, it should be explained, concern problems of individual American citizens as well as the issuance of visas to foreigners and the making of trade and economic reports. Embassies and legations deal with the central authorities on matters affecting broader governmental relations.

I avowed frankly to the minister that my service career had been limited to consular work and that the diplomatic side of the foreign service was completely unfamiliar to me. All I could assure him was that I would do my best. "Good," he replied with a smile. "We shall then sink or swim together. I can only offer you my own full cooperation," adding with a twinkle in his eye, "so far as that may be of any assistance." The words we exchanged bound me to him in a strong attachment during the two and a half years of our association.

To state that I was, for all Jardine's reassuring words, thoroughly dismayed at the new responsibilities so unexpectedly thrust upon me would be an understatement. I expressed my apprehensions to George, who laughed and made light of them. "It will not take you long to find your way around. Use your common sense. When a problem arises, have a look at the files for precedents and guidance. You needn't worry. There are a good many greater fools than you in our diplomatic service, even in the top ranks."

Fortunately for me, as well as for Jardine, American problems in Egypt in 1931 were relatively simple. The American colony, not exceeding fifty, included principally professors at the American University, archaeologists, missionaries, a few businessmen, and two American judges of the Egyptian Mixed Courts. Of these, the senior was Judge Pierre Crabitès of New Orleans, who had spent many years in Egypt. We became warm friends and he was an indispensable crutch until I gained my bearings and could walk confidently alone. My first task was to gain some knowledge of the background of the country and of its political problems. Economic and agricultural questions would devolve upon the commercial and agricultural attachés, representing then our Departments of Commerce and Agriculture.

If any country in the Near East has been a racial melting pot it is Egypt. Since gaining independence it has laid claim to being Arab, but no country of the Arab League of which it forms a part could be less so. Basically its people are Hamitic, together with a compound of Sudanese and Pharaonic blood, with an intermixture of Arabs who conquered the country in the seventh century, Greeks, and the Turkish latecomers, who extended their dominion over it as part of the Turkish Empire.

For an understanding of Egypt one must go back some years in its history. Early in the nineteenth century Mohammed Ali, an Albanian, after distinguishing himself with Turkish forces in Egypt, was named governor with the title of Pasha. A descendant purchased from the Sultan the title of Khedive. Britain's preoccupation with Egypt began to manifest itself with the opening in 1869 of the Suez Canal under a concession granted to Ferdinand de Lesseps. That originally French enterprise had drawn to Egypt a host of the financial vultures characteristic of the century. The Khedive's extravagant inclinations were given full rein with loans pressed upon him at ruinous rates of interest. With his virtual bankruptcy in 1875 it became necessary for him to sell to the British Government the 177,000 shares he owned in the canal. Five years later French interests acquired from the Egyptian Government its 15 per cent interest in the canal company's profits. It was not long before the annual return on this French investment was no less than the original amount paid for it, or the equivalent of about $5,000,000. Thus was alienated the last Egyptian financial interest in the canal. It was not until 1936 that the Egyptian Government was granted representation on the board of the canal company or that it came again to have any return from an enterprise which had yielded the West fantastic profits.

The original concession provided that 10 per cent of the dividends from the canal should accrue to the holders of founders' shares, which had been distributed by the company to some of the leading figures in Europe, and doubtless in Egypt also, for their influence in obtaining the concession and the establishment of the company. It is significant that the company persisted in refusing to make public the names of these shareholders. In a suit once brought against the company to that end a French court declined to act on the ground that "family secrets" were involved. It would be unjust to conclude that the corruption and financial stockjobbery of foreign interests in the second half of the last century in Egypt were peculiar to European nations; the United States was not above it as late as the 1920's in Central and South America. Nor are the facts offered as justifying the Egyptian Government's subsequent action in expropriating the canal. They do, however, help to explain it.

In 1881 Great Britain took the momentous step of occupying Egypt. The explanation offered in justification was the protection of law and order threatened by a nationalist uprising under Arabi Pasha, a prototype of Colonel Gamal Abdel Nasser. The real purpose was the protection of British investments, including in particular the Suez Canal, become by then the lifeline of the British Empire in its communications with India and the East.

From 1881 to 1914 Egypt continued to form a nominal part of the Turkish Empire, although ruled by a local dynasty under British occupation. This anomalous situation was not terminated until the declaration of a British protectorate over the country with the entrance of Turkey on the side of the Central Powers in the First World War. In 1922, in the face of an unprecedented tide of nationalist sentiment aroused by Wilson's principle of self-determination of nations and Lenin's appeal to Eastern peoples to free themselves from their imperialist regimes, Britain proclaimed the independence of Egypt subject to four reserved points. What they amounted to in practice was that while Egypt had the outward façade of independence, with a King and a constitutional government, the effective ruler of the country continued to be Great Britain.

If King Fuad maintained himself in oriental splendor at Abdin Palace, it was a British High Commissioner who pulled the strings governing the fundamental lines of both internal and external policy. If a Prime Minister ostensibly presided over the government, it was British advisers installed in most of the Ministries who directed the real machinery. It must be said that these were a consecrated group of men. In view of the preponderant role played by them in the affairs of Egypt, I made it a point to cultivate their acquaintance and formed warm friendships with John Besly in Justice, with Alexander Keown-Boyd (or K-B as he was known), director of Public Security, with Lynn Hugh-Jones in Finance, and with Horace Mayne in Communications. I was less successful in efforts to develop fruitful contacts at the British Residency. Until the Second World War, British diplomats looked upon their American colleagues in the Near East who sought to familiarize themselves with political problems as interlopers in an exclusively British domain. Walter Smart, British Oriental Secretary, with an unrivaled knowledge of the Egyptian political scene, was always gracious and friendly but as coy as a maiden being led to a bridal bed whenever I sought to turn the conversation to subjects other than the weather or the social life of Cairo.

British advisers were both less reserved as well as far more helpful than their fellow countrymen at the residency. I had initially looked upon the former as serving British interests exclusively. I was to find that I had been guilty of as great a misconception of their generally disinterested service as many unthinking Egyptians. Horace Mayne once described for me, with unconcealed glee, an interview he had had with Sir Percy Loraine, British High Commissioner, which illustrated the refusal of at least one adviser to subordinate Egyptian to British interests. Loraine summoned Mayne to account for his approval of specifications for a public tender by the Ministry of which he was the adviser without having consulted the commercial secretary of the residency. "Will you tell me, Mr. Mayne," the High Commissioner inquired, "why you failed to take such a measure which would have protected and been advantageous to British bidders?"

"Sir, I am an adviser not to the British but to the Egyptian Government. It is that government which pays my salary. I conceive it my duty to serve its interests so long as they are not in conflict with those of my own country."

My profound admiration for the loyal service these advisers generally gave the Egyptian Government was well deserved. They were for the most part men of high competence and of sterling integrity. There were, of course, deficiencies in the British administration of the country, at least it seemed so to an outsider on whom no responsibilities devolved. With primary emphasis on irrigation, finance, and security, it might have been argued that inadequate attention was given to education. There was also the matter of graft. The British were concerned with eliminating any squeeze of the *fellahin*, or peasants, but the more important dipping into the public till on the part of the King and his ministers tended to be ignored. It may have been that political considerations rendered any effort to eliminate graft at the top impractical or, then again, it may have been considered of too Augean a character or beyond the scope of their assignments.

The resolution I had formed to acquaint myself with Egyptians was put into execution soon after my arrival. It was initially furthered by an introduction my mother-in-law had given us to the head of one of the leading Coptic families, whom she had met on a prewar visit. Bakhoum Bey, locally know as "the Buddha of Shepheard's," where he held court in the lounge every afternoon, was one of the most fabulous and widely known figures in Cairo. Through him we were introduced to prominent Copts or Christian Egyptians. My wife had gone to school at Eastbourne in England with Sherifa Kurhan, of the Egyptian royal family, and through her our objective was further facilitated. In a few months we knew practically everyone of any importance in Cairo, as well as many not so important but of future promise. Far from being ostracized, we were welcomed everywhere. That the course I had followed was quite exceptional, however, was brought home to me when I was introduced to Mohammed Mahmoud Pasha, a graduate of Cambridge, a former Prime Minister, and leader of the Liberal Constitutional party. Taking my hand warmly in his, he remarked, "You need no introduction to me. I know all about you." Perceiving my bewilderment, he hastened to add, "You have become well known in Cairo as the first foreign diplomat who has made an effort to make friends with Egyptians."

It was about 1932 when our meeting occurred. On arriving in Cairo, I had found the lines drawn between the Anglo-Saxon and Egyptian communities as I had been given to expect in Bucharest. I had made a definite effort to bridge them. As I was only a second secretary, it had never occurred to me that my activities would excite attention. That they did was proof not only of how deep racial lines ran but also of the sensitiveness of Egyptians to them. Gezira Sporting Club, situated in the virtual center of Cairo, was a conspicuous and painful example. This great tract of land, with its golf and race courses and its many other amenities, was open to everyone of any social standing—with the sole exception of Egyptians. It is true that half a dozen of special prominence had been accepted, no doubt to avoid its being said that no Egyptian could gain admission.

If the British did not mix socially with Egyptians, there was no rush on the part of Americans to set a contrary example. The excuse generally offered was the deep difference in customs which divided Egyptians from the West. Thus, while Moslem men would accept invitations from Americans and Europeans, their wives were subject to the restrictive laws of the harem, preventing free and reciprocal social interchanges. This justification had some basis, but my feeling always was that it was exploited and served conveniently to cover the deep prejudice commonly entertained against Egyptians. Only one or two British residents made any effort to cultivate Egyptians socially, namely, John Besly and A. N. Williamson-Napier, a junior British diplomat who had the reputation of being something of an eccentric. With the outbreak of the Ethiopian crisis in 1935 the word went out that British Army messes as a matter of policy should entertain Egyptian officers. By that time such overtures were too transparent and much too late. It would be incorrect to attach undue importance to this British social prejudice as it manifested itself in Egypt. It seems fair to state, however, that the reserve maintained did not tend to promote Egyptian good will or a better understanding between Egypt and the West.

What a single individual could accomplish in this regard was brought home to me by an article by Stanley Parker, editor of the *Egyptian Gazette*, on January 5, 1934, the day of my departure from Cairo for Tehran, where I had been transferred. Reference was made in the most flattering terms to the role I had played as a diplomat in the life of Cairo. Once I had gained the confidence of Jardine, he had left the affairs of the legation almost wholly in my hands, as did his successor in 1933, Judge Bert Fish, political boss of Florida, a Roosevelt appointee. With Fish my relations had been no less happy than with Jardine. Apart from the interest Jardine had taken in agriculture, neither was concerned with the day-to-day work of the legation, with the result that I had been left a free hand and had been recognized, in fact if not in name, as the chief of the mission. The kudos and salary were sufficient compensation to Jardine and Fish. If I dwell on this in my own case, it should not be assumed that the circumstances were unusual; it was typical of many American diplomatic missions headed by political appointees.

If I had become, according to Parker's overly generous estimate, an "outstanding figure in Cairo," I had gained a somewhat different reputation with the State Department. In 1930–34 the world seemed on the point of falling about our heads. With a world economic depression the delicate economic and social fabric of Europe began to be torn asunder. Hoover's moratorium on war debts, at first hailed as the most important event since the 1918 armistice, appeared in retrospect like fighting a forest fire with a garden hose. Hitler was consolidating his power with the cold efficiency of an international gangster. There were warnings enough by able foreign correspondents in Germany, in particular those of the *Manchester Guardian*, whose weekly edition had become my Bible so far as foreign affairs were concerned, and there were the storm signals run up vainly by Americans such as William Shirer, John Gunther, and Edgar Scott Mowrer. The world's indifference was the most powerful accomplice of the Hitler regime. With the swift succession of the proclamation of a Spanish republic, a mutiny in the British Fleet, and suspension of the British gold standard, these events and others assumed for me an apocalyptic character portending the end of the world into which I had been born.

The lessons I drew from them moved me to write at almost white heat *Before the Curtain Falls*, published anonymously in the United States early in 1933. Despite extensive and favorable reviews sales were negligible, appearing as it did coincidentally with a grave American financial crisis. It mirrored immaturely the despair of many of us in the face of contemporary events which appeared to be dragging the Western world to a catastrophe which its leaders showed an incapacity to stay.

Had the book been published in the heyday of Joseph McCarthy, I might well have been separated from the service as a "premature antifascist." To be right at the wrong time has been one of my most persistent failings, together with an unwillingness to trim my sails when I felt the truth was involved. There was no concealment on my part of views I had formed as early as 1922 in Russia that the latent strength of that country was being seriously underestimated by the West. When Parker asked me for an anonymous review of Calvin B. Hoover's *The Economic Life of Soviet Russia* (1931) for the April 3, 1931, issue of the *Egyptian Gazette*, I wrote of how Lenin

enters Russia in 1917 from which he had been exiled and, without funds and with only a corporal's guard of followers, seizes power by his astute grasp of the realities of the situation, and becomes master of one-sixth of the earth's surface. Surrounded by armies of the victorious Great Powers he successfully frees Russia from the invaders and in the midst of the most indescribable economic disorganization, coolly formulates a tentative plan for the electrification of the country, its industrialization, and the mechanization of agriculture, a plan put on paper in 1920 under his direction with the hope of its being achieved in fifteen years and which is realized ten years later with an output of power stations four times that of pre-war and an industrial output double that of 1913. Declamations and embargoes have proved futile to stay the inexorable march of events in Russia.

There was a certain exaggeration here in that Lenin was certainly not without funds when he returned to Russia. What I sought to underline was that the country was going ahead and making progress. That was also the opinion of a few other men more expert than I. When Paul van Zeeland, an economist, later Belgian Prime Minister, visited Egypt on a financial mission in 1931 or 1932, we had long talks about the world situation. I sought his opinion of my thought that Russia might in time develop greater political freedom and we a more just economic regime. I was flattered that our views were not far apart. He saw Russia as far left of center, the West less off center to the right, with the two destined eventually to converge. He had visited Russia and had set forth his impressions in a short pamphlet *Reflections on the Five-Year Plan,* published in 1931, a copy of which he gave me.

In 1934 my opinions drew from the Department of State an expression of concern over charges that had been made that I was a Soviet sympathizer. It was suggested that I had displayed undue interest in events in that country. In my reply I stated that I considered it a part of my professional duties to follow developments in Russia as well as in Nazi Germany or wherever events were taking place which had explosive possibilities. I suggested that an effort to understand them did not necessarily imply any degree of sympathy. I was interested in the circumstances attending the burning of the Reichstag, but this did not warrant the deduction that I was an advocate of arson. There could be no gainsaying that my outlook was heretical. To intimate in the 1930's belief in the successful development of the Russian Five-Year Plan was to leave an implication of Communist sympathies as well as of skepticism about the "American way of life." The views I held never obtruded in the official discharge of my duties. If I reported the facts as I saw them, it was to serve rather than to subvert my country. I was constantly mindful of the counsel Prentiss Gilbert, one of our most brilliant career officers, had given me when I entered the service. "If you would be happy in your career, be prepared to serve cheerfully at any post and to report the truth as you see it, however disagreeable it may be to Washington."

Since entering the service I had made it a point to return home every two years in order not to lose touch with the United States. This I did notwithstanding the financial sacrifice involved: officers who took home leave did so at their own expense. In Bucharest we had contrived to cover the cost by renting our apartment and by proceeding from Constanţa for the three-week voyage to New York and return by a line which granted us a 50 per cent reduction in fare. Faced with the same problem in Egypt, we had taken ship in 1932 on an Isthmian freighter from Port Said at a cost of $42 each. We had been at sea en route to New York but two or three days when I received a telegram from the legation in Cairo that, for reasons of economy, foreign service salaries had been cut by 15 per cent and all leave taken was without pay. I refused to allow this to deflect me from my purpose of buying a car on arrival in order that we might have a close-up view of the United States, essential in the discharge of my official duties abroad. I borrowed the maximum available on my insurance and covered 8,500 miles to the West Coast and back in the twenty-three days available. By rigid economy we reduced our travel expenses in the United States to some $75 each.

Jardine had asked me to plumb the state of political opinion and report to him on the probable outcome of the forthcoming presidential election in November. If Roosevelt won, all political chiefs of mission would be obliged to tender their resignations. Wherever I stopped I dropped the remark, "I suppose all you people are voting for Hoover." The answer generally received, in one form or another, was, "Only those in insane asylums, mister." By the time we reached California I wrote Jardine that he might as well start packing his bags; Roosevelt would win by an overwhelming majority. The only contrary straws in the wind were in Reno, where the gamblers were offering two to one on Hoover, and in New York, where the bankers were convinced of a Republican victory.

VI

THE CHARM OF PERSIA

IN JANUARY 1934 when we set out from Cairo for Tehran the only means of reaching the Persian capital was overland. George Wadsworth had driven it in his own car when transferred there three years earlier. I decided to follow his example despite the risk of being stuck in the sand on a road but little frequented.

Other than being blocked by snow and obliged, in consequence, to follow a roundabout way from Beirut through Aleppo, Homs, and Hama, we encountered no particular difficulties until reaching Damascus. There, as it was clearly unsafe to drive alone to Baghdad, we engaged a chauffeur from a transport company and arranged to accompany one of its biweekly buses across the desert. We left one morning, drove all that day, and broke our journey midway at the desert post of Rutba. That night after dinner we continued on in inky blackness. As dawn broke we were vastly relieved to see in the distance the Euphrates. Soon we were on a paved road extending through Ramadi to Baghdad. We could relax and smile over our apprehensions of the previous night. They had not been unjustified, for in the past more than one car had been bogged down in the desert by mud or sand and its occupants lost through thirst or starvation before relief could reach them.

Baghdad possessed none of those ancient splendors associated with the capital of Harun-al-Rashid. It was dirty, dull, and down-at-the-heel, and a dispiriting rain, persisting for two days, in the end made it necessary for us to entrain with our car for Khanaqin, whence the Persian border might be reached thirteen miles farther. There customs authorities gave us our first insight into the scant consideration accorded foreign diplomats by Iranians. The minute examination of our effects could not have been more thorough if we had been criminals.

Ahead of us loomed the great Zagros mountain range, presenting a gloomy and forbidding appearance, accentuated by its barrenness. Soon we were making the tortuous ascent of the Pai-tak Pass through which Medes, Persians, Achaemenians, Sassanians, and other armies had defiled from the Persian plateau onto the Mesopotamian plain since the dawn of civilization. A memorial of one such passage was a Babylonian bas-relief dating from 2800 B.C. Snow had fallen to such a depth on the plateau that the road took the form of a canyon dug out by hundreds of laborers. It was only late in the evening after being extricated from a ditch into which the car had slid that we reached Kermanshah, 130 miles from Khanaqin. After resting up a day, we deemed it prudent to engage a chauffeur to remedy my complete ignorance of motors and to guard us from the pitfalls of the difficult road ahead.

There was an ominous grayness in the sky when we resumed our journey. The sight of trucks turned over in ditches along the way did nothing to reassure us. Soon we ran into a blinding snowstorm which so reduced visibility that the chauffeur had to run ahead of the car to indicate the way, and we were able to average no more than ten miles an hour. Late that afternoon, as we were proceeding for greater security behind a truck, it began to skid as it mounted the steep gradient of an icy hill, halting but inches from the edge of a deep precipice. To avert a collision I had put my gears in reverse, only to find myself skidding in turn but, happily, in the direction of a ditch rather than the ravine. My wife screamed with such force in Russian that her voice echoed in the hills. The driver of the truck, without pausing to take stock of his own dangerous predicament, rushed up to expostulate with her for not having disclosed sooner her knowledge of a language with which he, as many Persians in the north, was familiar. His reaction under the circumstances was so incongruous that, after having been transfixed with fear, we joined in fits of immoderate laughter. While debating whether to continue, a truck, emerging out of the darkness ahead, put an end to our discussion by informing us it would be folly to proceed.

A few miles earlier we had passed a primitive *chaikhani*, or teahouse, and we retraced our way to it. Crowded with drivers of snowbound trucks, it offered little cheer in our half-frozen state. A single private room was available, with two rickety beds and a smoking stove. Our fitful sleep that night was broken by rats running over our blankets in search of the crumbs left from our evening meal.

The next morning the continuing blizzard portended a disagreeable delay. We were long overdue in Hamadan and Tehran, and it was concluded by the legation staff that we had perished in the storm. Telegraphic inquiry on the part of my colleagues to the local governor, Farajollah Khan, brought them the news that we were lodged in the *chaikhani* and us an invitation to lunch. After hearing of our plight, he insisted that we go to the inn for such belongings as we might need and then return to be his guests until the storm lifted.

As we emerged from the governor's home, we were rudely halted by a youthful officer of the gendarmerie. He announced that I was under arrest and would be escorted back to Kermanshah to answer charges of illegal possession of firearms. In my absence from the inn he had spotted a pistol, which I had left exposed on the seat of my car, and had broken the lock of the car to gain possession of it. When I protested that I was immune from arrest, he professed ignorance of the functions and privileges of a diplomat or what a legation represented. When I suggested that he seek enlightenment of the governor with whom we had been lunching, he answered truculently that he was not under the governor's orders. Only after I made slighting reference to Persian discourtesy to foreigners, about which Near Eastern peoples are particularly sensitive, and a threat that his superiors in Tehran might take a somewhat gloomy view of his conduct was the question of my arrest dropped. In the end I even succeeded in obtaining a receipt for the impounded gun.

Two days later the snow stopped sufficiently to enable us to resume our way, and twenty-eight days after leaving Cairo, having covered 2,500 miles, we motored into the legation compound. The next year we returned by the same route in the summer in five days.

Upon reaching Tehran I expected Wadsworth, whom I was replacing, to make a vigorous protest to the government against the treatment I had received. George only smiled indulgently. "Your education in Persian ways is just beginning. You will be lucky to recover your pistol and to avoid a complaint by the Persian Foreign Office *against you*. As for any expression of regret, you can forget it. No Persian in history has ever been known to admit having made a mistake. Get a copy of Morier's *Hajji Baba*.[1] It will teach you more of the Persian mentality than I can tell you or than you can learn by yourself." George was right. I eventually had the pistol returned with no comment. He regarded the recovery of it as a notable diplomatic victory. After a few months in the country I came to the same conclusion.

If my assignment in Cairo had offered a challenge, in Tehran I was to mark time. My chief, a political appointee who arrived shortly after I, proved to be from a characteristic breed. Such men cannot conceive that career officers who have given their lives to the service can fail to resent the nomination of an outsider to head a post. As a consequence they assume that traps will be set to show up their shortcomings. They cannot believe that they may count on disinterested counsel.

It was so with "the great and good friend" whom Roosevelt had considered sufficiently worthy of his confidence to be named American Minister to Persia. The latter's lack of confidence in me was well exemplified on one occasion when he was to visit Afghanistan, where he was likewise accredited. On the evening of his departure the local representative of Thomas Cook called to exhibit a telegram he had received from the minister directing him to obtain the key of the legation from me in order to recover and expedite a code book left behind in one of the bedrooms. I informed my visitor, not without protest from him, that I had no intention of giving a foreigner access to the legation and that I would take the necessary measures as the officer responsible for the conduct of the legation in the minister's absence.

A further surprise awaited me the next day when I opened the chancery. The Armenian accountant, John Marelia, with visible embarrassment, disclosed that he had been instructed by the minister to render him a weekly report on the legation's activities during his absence. "In that case, John," I said, "You had better move your desk into my office in order that you may follow every development at first hand. When I go to the Foreign Office, you will accompany me and sit in on all conversations I have with the Foreign Minister or other officials."

"I couldn't possibly do that," John replied.

"Suit yourself, but don't mistake me. I am willing to give you every cooperation in the fulfillment of the instructions of the minister."

A few hours later John came, shamefacedly, to tell me that he was writing the minister he had found it beyond his capacity to make the reports he had requested.

The bad marks which he registered against me in Washington must have been discounted in the long run. At his next post an exasperated government was moved to request his recall under circumstances somewhat humiliating to him.

I must, however, do the minister justice. He may have made himself ridiculous on more than one occasion to his more experienced diplomatic colleagues and to the astute Persian officials, but he was above reproach in his personal conduct. The same could not be said of one of his Near Eastern colleagues, guilty of an offense probably unique in diplomatic annals. A jovial, hulking figure, grizzled and bronzed by the years, he conceived the novel idea for a foreign chief of mission of launching a house of prostitution in a city ill-supplied with such amenities. A dispute having arisen with his Persian partner, the ambassador had the effrontery to appeal to the Foreign Ministry and request the intercession of the Ministry of Justice for a settlement of his accounts. I would not have credited the story if it had not been recounted to me by a high official of the Foreign Office to whom the ambassador had addressed his complaint.

That foreign diplomat, a shrewd businessman, had taken into reckoning the almost complete absence in Tehran of normal distractions, apart from the Tehran Club, center of social life of the small foreign community. Aside from bridge playing a main preoccupation was the study and collection of Persian carpets, of which unusual pieces were still to be found. We had a windfall from the sale of a piano we had brought from Cairo quite unaware that pianos brought fabulous prices locally owing to the ban on their import by private individuals. We invested the proceeds in rugs, most of which were sold to us by an itinerant merchant, a Persian Jew, appropriately named Moses, who was so far honest in his dealings that he would frequently disclose the price he had paid for a carpet and smilingly announce that he was only asking us double. It was generally easily worth what he asked. We never paid more than a hundred dollars for any we purchased and oftentimes considerably less.

The local bazaars were also a fruitful source of art treasures to the discriminating. With my wife's knowledge of Chinese ceramics, she turned up a Ming jar and an early celadon vase of the greatest rarity. The latter's identity had been concealed under a coating of silver paint, but the exterior design had enabled her to detect its original character. The two, purchased for a song, had presumably found their way to Persia from China during the centuries of contact in the course of which Chinese artisans had been attracted to Persia to aid in the development of its art.

For my part I was busy assembling a collection of books on a country which absorbed me more and more as my knowledge of it grew. In the end I acquired several hundred volumes, including those of the many great European travelers from Britain, France, and Italy who have left fascinating accounts of Persia in the seventeenth, eighteenth, and nineteenth centuries. They now form a part of the American Embassy library in Tehran and perhaps will prove to be the most lasting contribution of my service there.

Because the minister early intimated that the less he saw of me the better, I was left with little to do but to pursue an independent study of the country. It was a double blessing: it enabled my wife and me to satisfy our love of travel by exploring every corner of a land of inexhaustible interest, and at the same time it removed us from the presence of one with whom we had nothing in common.

Of the eighty and more foreign countries and colonies I have visited, three stand out for me preeminently: France for its unsurpassed culture and amenities of living, Japan for the artistry it has introduced into life, and Persia for reasons which I find it difficult to define. To analyze its spell is as elusive a task as that of isolating the elements making up the indefinable charm of a woman. There is first of all its rose-tinted landscapes, comprising lofty barren mountains overlooking a succession of deserts and oases, the whole ringed by tropical vegetation in the north and south. From the life-giving water from snowfalls in winter on the central plateau, wistful gardens spring into being to which weeping willows and chinars impart a tender melancholy. Against this background, scattered throughout the country, are a succession of ancient monuments portraying the pageant of Persia's checkered past. Persian architecture, murals, ceramics, and textiles reflect the consummate artistic sense of the people. Side by side with the beauties revealed by nature are those fabricated by the hand of man.

The calendar of Persian glories would not be complete without mention of the literature, inclusive of the *Arabian Nights*. The poetry is without peer unless it be English poetry, which Persia has enriched through Edward Fitzgerald's adaptation of Omar Khayyam's *Rubáiyát*.

Noteworthy also are the religions Persia has given the world, including Zoroastrianism, not without influence on the sources of our own Christian faith; Mithraism; Mazdakism; Shi'ism, a branch of Islam; and Baha'ism.

It may be, however, that Persia's strongest magnet for us is in the affinities we find when returning to one of the earliest homes of our Aryan ancestors and our responsiveness to a land and people which shaped our roots thousands of years ago. The charm exercised by Persia on some of us may well have an element of atavism. It is altogether too profound to be explained by merely surface impressions.

To travel in Iran is to traverse one of the world's most impressive museums. Those who rush about as does the modern air traveler gain small appreciation of Persia. It must be done as we did—leisurely, by car, traveling with folding cots in order to be prepared to sleep out under the stars or in abandoned caravansaries which line many of the routes. It was thus that we visited Isfahan, with its exquisite bridges, palaces, and mosques, remnants of the Sefavid reign of Shah Abbas of the sixteenth and seventeenth centuries. Farther south was Shiraz, birthplace of Hafiz and Sadi, among the world's greatest poets, and intervening, Persepolis, where Dr. Ernst Herzfeld was laying bare an Achaemenian palace. In close vicinity were the tombs of Cyrus and of Darius and Xerxes, cut in solid rock, along with memorials left by the Sassanians and Parthians.

On a journey to Tabriz in the north we were rewarded by monuments of the Mongols who had conquered the land in the wake of Jenghiz Khan, leaving observatories, mosques, and colleges as testimonies that they were something more than destroyers. With the aid of the accounts of old travelers, assisted by the topographic knowledge of an American missionary, Christie Wilson, I succeeded in identifying, outside Tabriz, a heap of rubble and masonry foundations as the remains of Rashidiyah, constructed by Sultan Ghazan's great minister, Rashid-ud-Din in the thirteenth century. Archaeologists have subsequently accepted the identification—without acknowledgment.

Returning through troubled Kurdistan, west of Lake Rizaiyeh, and traversing a plateau region of savage grandeur, we were pushing on after twilight when, in the gathering darkness, a figure brandishing a rifle suddenly loomed up in the center of the road. During that afternoon occasional Kurdish nomads had passed us; we had no doubt that we were in for trouble. To our relief the man whom we had mistaken for a bandit was an Iranian soldier who informed us that, owing to prevailing insecurity, no travel was permitted through Kurdistan after dark. There was nothing to do except to spread our cots under the trees lining the road at the outskirts of the village we had reached.

On another occasion, in the company of Sidney Simmons of the British Legation and his American wife, a talented artist, we made the long journey to the desert cities of Yezd and Kerman in the extreme southeast. One of our principal objectives was the Moslem shrine at Mahan, an architectural gem in an oasis twenty miles east of Kerman. Beside it was a great tiled pool whose waters mirrored the delicate graceful outlines of the shrine. On every side were weeping willows, extending their branches as if in protection of a site of such ethereal beauty. When I later saw the Taj Mahal, it left me cold in the light of my recollections of Mahan. I shall never return to have the spell it cast over me altered. It was bitter sweet in its incomparable beauty.

A part of the spell cast by Persia springs from the reminder it everywhere offers of man's transitoriness and tragic destiny. These are reflected in its memorials, many in ruins, to those who ruled for a brief space only to give way to other dynasties. It explains the turn of men's minds to religion, mysticism, and philosophy. With examples on every hand of the decay of man's most majestic works, along with the depredations of nature in the perpetual encroachment of the desert on the cultivated oases, nature conspires with man to induce an absorption in man's fate. Nowhere is it more poignantly set forth than in Persian poetry, of which the *Rubáiyát* is a characteristic example:

> Oh, come with old Khayyam, and leave the Wise
> To talk: one thing is certain, that Life flies;
> One thing is certain, and the Rest is Lies:
> The Flower that once has blown for ever dies.

Considerations such as these explain why time does not have the same significance for the Persians as for us. Innumerable invaders have passed over the land: Alexander, Jenghiz Khan, Tamerlane, Seljuks, Arabs, and Russians, but none have left a permanent impress. Sultans and shahs have risen, reigned briefly, and been shorn of their glory. "Thou hast seen Alp Arslan's head exalted to the sky. Come to Merv and see how lowly in the dust that head doth lie." Everything is transitory. Nothing presses when all is momentarily subject to change.

Of these sudden transformations of fortune no more striking

example was to be had than the reigning monarch, Reza Shah Pahlevi, founder of a dynasty. It was my privilege to be presented formally to him in his fairylike palace of Gulistan. He had begun life as an uneducated soldier, rising by the sheer strength of his personality to colonel. When effecting the overturn of the effete Kajar dynasty in 1921, he had engineered a *coup d'état*, with the blessing of the British and had assumed control. Given to few words and entirely lacking in polish, he was a cold, forbidding figure, with eyes of steel and a stiff military carriage which reflected an indomitable will.

If the Persian resembles the Frenchman in wit and cultivation of mind, he is akin to the German and Russian in his amenability to the mailed fist. Throughout history Persian rulers have maintained their power by the exercise of ruthless force; they fell with any least relaxation in their despotic sway. No one knew the character of his people better than Reza Shah Pahlevi. So terrorized were his ministers that they lived in constant apprehension of imprisonment or execution. When a modern prison was built in Tehran, the diplomatic corps was conducted through it by Taymurtash, principal minister of the Shah and a man of outstanding capacity. To the corps he confided that he had taken special pains to see that the prison was provided with every modern amenity. "Why not?" he wryly observed, "I may be an inmate myself one day." Twelve months had not expired before he was the occupant of a cell, and not long thereafter he was dead, strangled, so it was said, by the Shah's own hand.

I visited the prison a little later with a group of Persian students under the aegis of Herrick Young from the American College. One of these asked the governor, unaware of my identity, if he had had to contend with any mass-organized escapes as in the United States. "We are a backward people," he smilingly answered. "Criminals in Persia do not have the advantage of American civilization." Inquiry was made if political prisoners might receive visits from friends. The governor's eyes twinkled as he parried: "Have you ever known a political prisoner to have a friend?"

The rise to power of Reza Shah was symptomatic of the awakening of the Near East from the lethargy of centuries. Mustapha Kemal had led the way with the conviction which was spreading that, to survive, ancient ways must be fundamentally overhauled. I witnessed the passing of many of these under my eyes. Such was that of the *kalaad*, or bestowal of a robe as a mark of favor by the Shah. It was a custom of which the Book of Esther records an example, where it is written that "for the man whom the King delighteth to honor, let the royal apparel be brought which the King useth to wear." It was abandoned by Reza Shah, but I found it prevailing in 1946 in Saudi Arabia.

Two other equally ancient ceremonies underwent drastic modification. One was the sending of a deputation to greet the arrival of a distinguished visitor, the other to accompany him on his departure. Today when the President welcomes a foreign chief of state at the Washington airport, he is observing, in a simplified form, a tradition observed by our Aryan ancestors, once so surrounded by such formality that the prescriptions concerning it were at times incorporated in treaties.

The sweeping reforms introduced by Reza Shah extended to liberalization of the status of women in permitting their unveiling and in giving them the right to enter restaurants and other public places and to speak to men in the streets. Legal procedure, previously subject to Koranic interpretation, was modernized, and the power of the Moslem clergy was drastically curbed in many other ways. Certain religious observances of pagan origin were eliminated, including the annual flagellation rites, as well as the Feast of Sacrifice, celebrated on the last day of the pilgrimage to Mecca. On that occasion it had been customary to sacrifice a male camel by a master of ceremonies known as King of the Day. When I witnessed the last performance of this ritual in 1934, I recognized it, on the testimony of James Frazer's *The Golden Bough* (1890), as of the highest antiquity, with survivals until modern times in some isolated parts of Europe. Two years later, on my return to Egypt, I was witness to a no less ancient observance during the funeral of King Fuad. When the procession approached the mosque at the foot of the Citadel, where his body was being borne, the throats of a number of bulls were slit till their blood ran in rivulets under our feet. It passed for a propitiatory offering to Allah in conformity with the Koran, but actually it was a ceremony dating from ancient times.

Along with the reforms looking to the westernization of the country, the Shah, inconsistently erected rigid barriers between his subjects and foreigners. If, in Egypt, it was the foreigners who interposed bars between themselves and the natives, in Persia the tables were turned. The only Persian officials permitted social intercourse with the diplomatic corps, which largely made up the foreign colony, were members of the cabinet and officials of the Foreign Ministry. The impediments thus imposed by the Shah were aimed at restricting intrigues on the part of Britain and Russia. For two centuries Persia had been a pawn in a struggle for domination between Great Britain and Russia.

Resistance to that struggle had long been a matter of wits rather than arms. The Persian is anything but martial in character, resembling in this respect the Italian. It may be that the high civilization of both has attenuated their combativeness. The attitude of the Persian is admirably reflected in a remark of the immortal Hajji Baba, who, when asked why the Persians did not stand up better in battle, replied that "we would all be brave if there were no question of dying."

If the Persian has little taste for murdering his fellowmen under government sanction, he possesses cultural aptitudes which distinguish all classes. When I encountered truck drivers and muleteers congregated in a teahouse or caravansary, their principal distraction was in the recitation of verses of their greatest poets: Firdausi, Hafiz, and Sadi. Not for them a banal discussion of sports or the exchange of off-color stories, which would mark the intellectual limits of their Western counterparts. Our two houseboys, when not quoting poetry to one another, busied themselves in drawing and painting with a talent ingrained in them and their people.

This cultural heritage runs so deep that it has left its imprint even on alien conquerors. An acute observer, E. Phillips Price, has written: "The Persian is always being conquered by the sword, but in turn always subdues the conqueror by his intellect." [2] When overrun by the Arabs and compelled to accept Islam, the Persian developed his own Shi'a sect, adapted to his own particular ways. Of all the Moslem countries it is Persia which most frequently ignores Koranic injunctions against the use of fermented drinks owing to a deeply rooted individualism.

Social reforms introduced by Reza Shah went hand in hand with measures to strengthen central authority and the economy. The power of the tribes was broken, while textile and sugar factories, of prime importance to the consumer, were established. With a view to extending the government's authority, the country's first railroad was constructed from the Persian Gulf to the Caspian Sea. The

north-south direction given it was dictated by a desire to free
northern Persia from its economic dependence on Russia. By a
curious irony, it had hardly been completed when it came to serve
Russia more than Persia as the main Allied supply route to the Soviet
Union during the Second World War.

During my stay in Persia, British influence was still paramount. It
was exercised through the British-controlled and staffed Imperial
Bank of Persia, the Persian Gulf, which was virtually a British lake,
and, more particularly, by the Anglo-Persian Oil Company. An oil
concession, obtained in 1901 by William Knox D'Arcy, in which the
British Government had acquired a controlling interest in 1914, had
thereafter tended to constitute something of an *imperium in im-
perio*. So great was the company's influence during my stay that the
prestige and position of the resident manager in Tehran, T. L. Jacks,
fell little short of that of the British Minister, Sir Hugh Knatchbull-
Hugessen. It was perhaps inevitable that this situation should finally
prove insupportable to Iran.

In 1934 I had occasion to call on Sir Hugh when I was acting as
chargé d'affaires and he had returned from a visit to the Persian
Gulf in connection with certain revisions of British political arrangements in that area. The British Minister was disposed to take a
lofty tone toward me. "And what may I ask can be the interest of
the United States in the Persian Gulf?" I had to be quick with an
answer which would be both convincing and calculated to temper
his toploftiness. "My government cannot but be interested in any
development affecting peace in any part of the world."

It is some measure of the change which has taken place in the
quarter of a century since that a United States Navy Persian Gulf
Command is now permanently stationed in the Persian Gulf and that
both the Imperial Bank and the Anglo-Persian Oil Company have
been liquidated in Iran. These developments are recorded, not with
any particular satisfaction on the part of an American, but to
indicate something of the revolutionary transformation of a country
where Britain and Russia once stood as protagonists and where now
the United States and the Soviet Union confront one another.

My travels about the country provided useful background material for an exhaustive study of Soviet-Persian relations from 1917 to
1935 which I based on the books I had collected and on the rich files
in the legation's archives.[3] When submitted to Washington, my

study formed a report of more than three hundred pages. What impression it made I never learned.

Among my conclusions was that the struggle between communism and capitalism would find its most important theater in the East and that it was there rather than in Western Europe that the destiny of our world might be decided.[4] Some of the material was later embodied in *The Pageant of Persia*, published under the pen name of Henry Filmer in 1936. In that work, paraphrasing my report, I wrote: "On the larger stage of the Middle and Near East . . . national-liberation movements, unleashed by the influence of the Russian Revolution, have created more formidable problems than imperialism has ever had hitherto to face." I added that there was no reason to believe there had been any change in the Soviet conviction that the forces set in motion by Leninism might not have the convulsive repercussions in the East which Lenin had envisaged when he saw in Western domination of that area the Achilles heel of capitalism.[5] No gift of prophecy was needed to foreshadow the future course of development of Soviet policy in the Middle East and East; it was limned in Soviet doctrine so clearly that even those who ran might read. The pity was that there were so few readers.

VII

TWO REVOLUTIONS

IN THE summer of 1935 the secretary of the Egyptian Legation, on friendly terms with my minister's daughter, confided to me that my chief was pressing Washington for my transfer. Although I found it curious to learn of this in such a manner, it came as no surprise. I had been associated with the minister only a month or two when he suggested that it was a pity for me to be wasting my "talents" at Tehran and that I would be wise to apply for a transfer. His discomposure was thoroughly amusing when I replied that my wife and I were quite happy in Persia and had no desire to leave it.

He must have been equally upset when, almost coincidentally with the measures he was taking to sever my connection with the legation in Tehran, I was notified of a promotion and, a few days later, of my reassignment to the legation in Cairo. This third promotion in some twelve years was not in itself breath-taking, but the prospect of returning to Cairo, which had taken on exceptional importance with the Italo-Ethiopian War, was enough to give me a heady feeling.

As we had been absent from Egypt only since January 1934, our return there in August 1935 was something of a homecoming. With the minister on leave in the United States, I assumed charge of the legation and set to work to assess a situation about which the Department of State was clamoring for information. Questions which were uppermost included whether the Suez Canal would be closed to Italy, what action the British Fleet, assembled in unaccustomed numbers in Alexandria, might be prepared to take, and whether Egyptian nationalists would exploit the international situation to extort concessions from Britain.

John Besly arranged for me to meet Gerald Kelley, British chargé, at an evening picnic in the desert. I learned much from John but Kelley, a charming and capable diplomat, was as discreet and reserved as an oyster. I spent an evening with Nokrassy Pasha, whose ostracism by the British for his alleged implication in Sir Lee Stack's murder in 1924 had not caused me to rebuff the overtures he had made me during my previous tour of duty. He was himself later, as Prime Minister, to fall under an assassin's bullet and his services as a nationalist leader to be commemorated in an imposing mausoleum. Nokrassy disclosed that Egyptian nationalist policy would take every advantage of the dilemma in which Britain found itself vis-à-vis Mussolini and the rising Hitler. I spent a fruitful afternoon at the country home of one of the ablest members of the cabinet, Abdul Wahab Pasha, with whom I had previously formed intimate contact.

The most profitable of my soundings was in the garden of Groppi's popular café with Abdul Rahman el Azzam. I listened for two hours as he reviewed the situation and then put this question to him: 'Surely the nationalists will not play into fascist hands by promoting disorders to extort full independence and add to Britain's embarrassment?" Azzam's eyes twinkled as he fingered his amber beads. "That is precisely what we shall do unless the British make immediate concessions. We are fed up with their promises. In the absence of concrete offers you will see rioting in Cairo in three weeks."

Subsequently I surveyed the international factors affecting Egypt. British policy toward Egypt, as well as toward the Italo-Ethiopian conflict, was a cautious, temporizing one of wait-and-see. British military men in Egypt were generally convinced that Mussolini had effectively transformed Italian armed forces into such powerful instruments that British naval and air units in the Mediterranean might be no match for the new weapons the Fascists had developed. There was also a deep-seated fear that if Mussolini were checkmated social upheavals in Italy might pave the way for communism there. As for the Suez Canal, treaties in force made it impossible to close it to Italian communications with Ethiopia short of a blockade. France was reluctant to go along with Britain out of pique at the Anglo-German Naval Treaty concluded in 1934 behind France's back. For Britain to establish a blockade independent of France and the League of Nations might mean war with Italy.

In retrospect it is clear that if Britain had taken a firm stand, Mussolini's Ethiopian adventure would have collapsed. If the Italian Fleet had resisted, it would have been swept from the seas by the more than eighty units of the British Fleet massed at Alexandria. If the Italian challenge had been met, it is extremely unlikely that Germany would have dared provoke war in 1939. In 1935 Eberhard von Stohrer, the German Minister, assured me that if the League adopted sanctions against Italy Germany would not dispute them. Germany would export no more and no less to Italy than in normal times. Hitler's policy was also one of wait-and-see in order to observe which way the wind might blow. When it blew hot and then cold, he took his cue and decided that he had nothing to fear from powers as irresolute as France and Britain.

My survey completed, I entrained for Alexandria to confer with Consul General H. Earl Russell there. The typing of a seventeen-page despatch embodying my conversations and conclusions, as I have set them forth, was completed as the train pulled into my destination. In the absence of airmail it passed over the desk of William Phillips, Under Secretary of State, three weeks later. That morning Phillips had read a copy of the New York *Times* announcing the outbreak of riots in Cairo the previous day. Phillips was handsome in his acknowledgment. I was formally commended for "the excellent manner" in which the information had been presented. I was also informed that "the despatch has proved of distinct assistance to the Department in gaining an understanding of the course of developments in Egypt." [1]

The Italo-Ethiopian War and the disorders provoked in Egypt had attracted to Cairo some famous American correspondents including an old friend, Floyd Gibbons, and a new one, Vincent (Jimmy) Sheean. Floyd was the hard-boiled type, given to sensationalism, who would blow up a riot into a revolution. Jimmy Sheean, on the contrary, for all the knowledge he had acquired in his wanderings, retained a virginal outlook on the world, as if spellbound by all he saw.

We frequented the popular night clubs, the open-air Kit-Kat and the Brasserie des Pyramides in the outskirts and the Continental cabaret in town, while I helped them in other ways to get the feel of the country. I introduced Jimmy to one of the most culturally gifted hostesses in Cairo, Maria Riaz (whose poetry was signed Maria Cavada), a Rumanian I had met in Bucharest who was given to changing husbands as lightly as trains, who entertained such divergent visitors as André Malraux and Barbara Hutton, and who cast her intellectual spell over Sheean as over everyone who came within her orbit. I overcame the reluctance of Keown-Boyd, virtual Minister of the Interior, to receive Floyd Gibbons, in disfavor for his sensational reporting. Gibbons gave me no peace until the meeting had been arranged. Anticipating a relentless catechism on his

Berber women, Valley of Dadès, Morocco, in 1941

A Berber at market near El Kelâa, Morocco, in 1941

part, I listened with mingled bewilderment and fascination while Floyd launched into a monologue about his experiences as a war correspondent.

I was sent to Shanghai in 1932 as soon as the Japs landed marines there. I was keeping three stenographers busy in relays when I had a peremptory cablegram from my office one day early in March. I took one look at it and said to everybody: "Well, folks, that will be all. We are packing up and going home."
"What's happened?" someone asked.
"Lindbergh's baby's kidnapped, that's all. The best this war will get from now on will be a few paragraphs on an inside page. . . . That's news for you."

And that was all that came out of our call on K-B, who probably knew more about the Egyptian situation than anyone else in the entire country, not excepting the King, the Prime Minister, or the British High Commissioner.

During the remainder of 1935 and the beginning of 1936 the Egyptian political situation was moving in the direction which had been forecast by Nokrassy and Azzam. Rioting and other civil disturbances assumed such proportions that Great Britain was compelled, in the end, to yield to the storm. Announcement was made of that government's willingness to enter into negotiations looking to the granting of full-fledged independence to Egypt with but one limitation—reservation of the right to garrison Cairo and the Suez Canal. Eighteen years later, in 1954, with the winds of change sweeping over the world and under accumulating Egyptian pressure promoted by American policy, Britain was moved to withdraw, with deep and justified misgivings, its last remaining forces in Egypt, those in the Canal Zone. This terminated a British connection with Egypt that promoted stability and that had lasted almost one hundred years.

Our responsibility in this was a heavy one. Self-determination of peoples was a principle Wilson had enunciated as one of the Fourteen Points. It had been conceived more particularly with reference to the Austro-Hungarian Empire, to Czechs and Hungarians in an advanced stage of political development. In the years that followed its application came to be extended to colonial possessions comprising peoples with limited, if any, capacity for self-government. Our anticolonial policy had two main inspirations. The first was our own struggle for independence as colonies. A sympathy thus sentimentally evoked persuaded us thereafter not to be displaced as a champion of the so-called oppressed when Soviet Russia began to appeal to colonial peoples to throw off their chains.

When we examine closely our assimilation of anticolonialism in the modern world with our anticolonial struggle in the Revolutionary War, certain fallacies and incongruities are revealed. We had a social development comparable to that of the Mother Country and were of the same blood. There is no proper parallel between our struggle for independence and that of quite undeveloped peoples, some but little removed from savagery and generally unequipped for self-government. Moreover, our treatment of the native Indian population gave us small title to call in question the colonial policies of other nations. The subject peoples within our borders were either massacred or herded into reservations with no civic rights given them. Yet our record did not give us pause when we advocated self-government for peoples in Asia and Africa, often in an even more primitive stage of development than the Indians. We have applied what we have mistakenly conceived as a lesson from our own history, and in doing so we have aligned ourselves with Russia in the espousal of a common objective, termed by us *anticolonialism* and by them *antiimperialism.*

In Egypt the British, with a somewhat greater sense of realism than we, were less blinded by illusions about the magic virtues of parliamentary democracy for non-Anglo-Saxon peoples without the thousand-year-old traditions behind them of Magna Carta. The British granted Egypt parliamentary government in 1922 in accordance with the popular fetish of the times, while preserving a wholesome skepticism of its efficacy in Egypt. In operation it was as much of a farce as I had found it to be in Rumania. If it had any virtue, it was that of a toy to distract an immature people. In the end it became an instrument for the dictatorial rule of Sidky Pasha, Prime Minister during most of the time I spent in Egypt, who governed with no popular support.

In the administration of Egypt the British relied upon that time-honored principle of divide and rule. The party commanding overwhelming support in the country was the Wafd, led by Nahas Pasha, whose single aim was the freeing of Egypt from the British. King Fuad entertained no illusions as to how his dynasty would fare if the people came to power. To keep the Wafd in check the British would tip the balance in favor of the Palace to bring Sidky into office; when the Palace tended to get out of hand, the Wafd was always a sword to be held over the King's head. The system worked effectively as long as there was a sovereign of some force and intelligence. With the succession of Farouk in 1936 and his subsequent enthronement when he came of age, the balance of political forces was radically upset. After the withdrawal of British forces from Cairo in 1951 and Farouk's alienation of every element of Egyptian public opinion by his corruption and irresponsibility, he was left isolated, with neither foreign nor domestic support to sustain him. The way was open for the Revolution of 1952 and the advent of the masses to power in the persons successively of Mohammed Naguib and Gamal Abdel Nasser. History had turned full circle. Colonel Arabi's revolt in 1881, which had occasioned British occupation of Egypt, had been completed by another representative of the peasantry or *fellahin* once British power was withdrawn. The old regime of the pashas, many of aristocratic Turkish blood and gentlemen to their fingertips, was ended.

The broad lines of the Revolution as it subsequently developed was prefigured in its essential outlines in a despatch I had drafted for the minister's signature on June 1, 1932. In it I observed:

There exists all the elements of a situation remarkably comparable to that which preceded the retirement of Primo de Rivera in Spain and the subsequent collapse of the power of the Spanish King. The distinctive difference, and that which alone makes it hazardous to venture upon pressing the analogy too far, is that of the position of Great Britain in Egypt and the support given the Palace and the Cabinet by an Egyptian Army and Egyptian police controlled by British officers. Only the fear of a violent outbreak against the present veiled dictatorship. [of Prime Minister Sidky Pasha] with the consequent intervention of Great Britain, and the possible reestablishment of a protectorate, keeps in leash popular forces and a sullen and increasingly resentful public opinion.[2]

There was no question but that a revolution in Egypt was long overdue. I had seen the wake of one in Russia; I was shortly to observe another in Spain; and I witnessed the development of one in Egypt. Before 1952 there was probably no other country of the world where the inequalities were comparable to those in Egypt. Between the masses, on the one hand, living in grinding poverty and the pasha class, flaunting an ostentatious luxury, the gulf was stark and pitiless. Between the two wars, the pashas and princely families, which were numerous, along with most of the foreign residents led a life akin to that of maharajas. Many rich Egyptians kept open house where guests, as in Russia before the Revolution, were welcome to lunch or dine without prior invitation. Receptions for six or seven hundred people, in spacious palaces or on well-kept lawns facing the Nile, were commonplace. Delicacies of every kind were in abundance, including the finest wines and champagnes. In fairly close proximity an undernourished population lived in filth and squalor. Ruling the country was a titular sovereign and his ministers but few of whom, and least of all the King, suffered compunctions about squeezing millions through corrupt practices from the masses.

Many foreigners and even some thoughtful Egyptians of substance were alive to the injustice of it all. There was, however, singularly little premonition, at least not expressed, that the regime would disappear in another twenty years. I never remember hearing the observation, "This cannot last." The fact was accepted by the lowliest Egyptian that no effective revolution was possible so long as British armed forces were installed in Cairo. Actually it was but a few brief months after the withdrawal of British forces from the city to the strictly limited zone of the Suez Canal that King Farouk was swept incontinently from his throne.

Much before this, on July 17, 1936, violence erupted at the opposite end of the Mediterranean in Spain. Earlier that summer I had been stricken with diphtheria on the eve of embarking for a month's leave in Europe, the first I had had in four years. For my convalescence I was generously accorded five months. Moved by insatiable curiosity, I decided to utilize part of the respite allowed me to observe something of the Spanish conflict at first hand. For that purpose I embarked for France in August with my car.

When I had in part regained my strength, I headed for Hendaye. Opposite Hendaye, Spanish republican and nationalist forces were struggling, the former to defend, their opponents to gain possession of, Irun. With a diplomatic passport I had no difficulty in obtaining a French pass permitting entry into the frontier zone where admittance was restricted to the population resident there, journalists who had been sent to observe the fighting in the area, and others who could justify their presence.

The small Bidassoa River flowed along the frontier. Perched on a bluff on the French side, not far distant, was the village of Biratou, reported to be the best vantage point for observation of the fighting.

The site commanded a full view of rolling meadows on the opposite, Spanish side, where forces of the two adversaries were in intermittent combat. There was a road which skirted the river from Behobie, just west of Hendaye, offering access to Biratou. Traversing it was not without danger because from time to time stray bullets whistled over or fell in its immediate vicinity. There was, however, no other way of reaching Biratou by car. From Behobie, accompanied by a famous French journalist, Marcelle de Jouvenel, whom I had met earlier in Egypt, I headed for my objective over a tortuous up-hill road as fast as my car could be driven under such circumstances. In a quarter of an hour I was safely through.

The terrace of a restaurant in Biratou offered a full view of the combat taking place only a few hundred yards opposite. It was fairly full with a score of journalists and a number of military attachés from the Madrid embassies. I was struck by its resemblance to the loge of a theater from which spectators might follow the play's action on the stage beyond and beneath. Shells were being lobbed intermittently from nationalist gun emplacements, within our vision, into the valley to the right, up which I had ascended. An armored train bearing the initials U.H.P. (Union of Proletarian Men), moving back and forth on a railway spur, was replying.

At length, a number of us, including Madame de Jouvenel, walked down, under cover of buildings along the way, to a point from which a view could be had of the railway track. Some in the group were preparing to take photographs when there was a warning burst of rifle fire while a voice shouted in French from the train demanding to know who we were. "Journalists," was the reply. "Have you any message for us?" was the next inquiry. "We are friends. What is your situation?" "One of confidence and fearlessness." There was a pause and then a request was shouted that we go to Biratou, return, and report the situation of the enemy. As no one fancied such a task, we left to regain the restaurant terrace.

After lunch the waitress advised me to return to Hendaye on foot through the fields as the road I had come by was too dangerous. Not wishing to abandon my car, I proceeded with Mme de Jouvenel back to the edge of the village, placed car seats on either side of our shoulders for such protection as these offered, and, after waiting for a lull in the fighting, stepped on the accelerator. There was the whine of a few stray bullets, but the international bridge between Behobie and Irun was reached without mishap.

A stream of refugees was crossing the bridge into France from Irun. Movement was all in the one direction until I spied a lone figure who presented himself to a French gendarme on the French side. He was a young man, coatless and hatless, without baggage and obviously of the working class. When his passport was found in order, he hesitated and began waving his arms in his agitation, half choking on the words he was trying to voice. The Bidassoa was his Rubicon; he felt the need of justifying himself in the step he was taking. He brushed his lips with the back of his hand and waved toward Irun. "The struggle there, it's not Spanish only. It's mine." He turned to the gendarme, "Will you have a glass before I go across?" "I'm sorry," the gendarme answered softly, "it's against the rules." With that the little man, his shirttail flopping grotesquely behind him, headed for Irun as a volunteer in the first armed struggle against fascism. As we watched him, there was a long hissing noise followed by a dull thud marking the passage of a shell which had failed to explode in Irun.

The next day I went down to the docks to observe a French ship arriving with refugees from Bilbao and fell into conversation with a young Frenchman, Jean Ehrhard, who had been teaching in Spain. He was eager to visit Barcelona to observe what was happening on the republican side. I fell in with his proposal that we drive there in my car. It was a foolhardy enterprise, but I had a consuming curiosity about a struggle which represented for me, as for the Frenchman I had seen the preceding day, the initial conflict between two worlds.

Before heading for Barcelona, we drove to the international bridge in the hope of having a look around Irun. On reaching the Spanish side of the bridge, we were halted by a republican militiaman who regarded us coldly. "Irun is no place for foreigners." Observing our disappointment, he added: "It's our place to be here. We are young and we can die fighting for something worth while. We accept the risk and expect to be killed but with you it's different." I remarked to Ehrhard in English: "There's a restaurant up there. Let's ask if we can go for a drink. If he refuses we can hang around and slip away when he is not looking."

The militiaman turned on me a sardonic and far from friendly smile. "I wouldn't do that," he observed in perfect English. He slapped his gun. "We had a foreigner here a few days ago who came across from France and wanted to go to San Sebastian. That's what he said. He didn't tell us that he was one of Franco's spies. He displayed a Hungarian passport. It was funny, wasn't it, that he couldn't speak a word of Hungarian but only German. Not exactly regular, was it? He also asked to go to that restaurant. I told him he couldn't. He hung around for a while and when he thought I was not looking he made a run for it." He slapped his gun again, "He never got to San Sebastian; he never even got as far as the restaurant." He slapped his gun once more and winked.

"You are quite a polyglot," I remarked, "speaking English, Spanish, French, Hungarian, and German. Where did you learn your English?"

He thrust his head forward so close to mine that I had to step back. "My friend, I have seen so much since July 17 that I can't remember much about my life before then." He laid his hand on mine revealing the emblem of the hammer and sickle engraved on a ring.

Pointing to it, I remarked that it was a Communist device. He broke into a flood of Spanish as he pointed to the ring with one hand and grasped my arm with the other. With a vehemence which startled me he shouted: "No, it's more than that. . . . It represents everything I live for, everything, do you understand?"

It was a spirit that animated large numbers of the Spanish republicans. Their fanaticism was matched only by that of the nationalists. It was a fanaticism which was to tear Spain apart and, ultimately, the greater part of Europe.

Ehrhard and I left at dusk on the evening of September 1, driving along the French Pyrenees to the Col de la Perche, where the French customs officials shook their heads wonderingly at our intention to cross into Spain. On the opposite side of the bridge there we were conducted before a committee of the Popular Front, surrounded by a group of heavily armed youth of both sexes hardly out of their teens, starry-eyed with their romantic vision of a world which was to be shattered in the defeat of the Republic. After minute examination of every scrap of paper we possessed, we were permitted to proceed to nearby Puigcerdá to await a decision by a higher committee whether we should be allowed to continue on to Barcelona. Authorization having been accorded us, we were provided with passes under the seal of the Puigcerdá authorities. Without them we could not have passed from one town to the next so strict was the surveillance.

Wars and revolutions bring to most minds deserted fields and towns seething with disorder. The reality is far more prosaic. With man's infinite capacity for adjusting himself to any situation, life goes on at much the same tempo as in normal times. The country-side and towns we traversed presented no unusual appearance except for the presence of armed militiamen at the entrance and exit of settled habitations and occasionally at churches, which were some-times intact and sometimes in ruins but always surmounted by the black and red flag of the Catalonian anarchists.

Upon reaching Barcelona in the early afternoon, we found the streets deserted; the civil war had introduced no alteration in the traditional Spanish siesta. By five the city was teeming with militia-men and workers. Requisitioned private cars and taxis bearing hast-ily painted initials of various political groups, F.A.I., P.S.U.C., and P.O.U.M., were rushing through the streets with heavily armed youths of those organizations. The first was the Federation of Anarchists of Iberia, strongest by reason of the Catalonian leaning toward anarcho-syndicalism, the second the Union of Socialists and Communists, and the third a left-wing group of Trotskyites. The conflicts brewing between these left-wing groups may have played a decisive part in the defeat of the Republic in 1939.

Apart from the militiamen the most distinguishing feature of the crowds was their dowdy appearance. Men in civilian clothes were generally coatless and hatless, and there was not a smartly dressed woman to be seen. It was a faithful image of Moscow in 1921 except that in Barcelona there was no dearth of merchandise in the shops. The brilliant night life for which it had once been notorious, with its elegant bordels, had disappeared. The most famous of its assigna-tion houses was now the headquarters of the P.S.U.C. A curfew was in force from midnight to dawn.

Anticipating far greater difficulty in leaving Barcelona than we had experienced in entering it, our first move was to obtain such permission at the headquarters of the Antifascist Militia of the Popular Front. An interminable queue was ahead of us, but the display of my diplomatic passport gave us immediate entry. A young man in an enormous office gave us a friendly welcome. He was about to stamp our passports when he was interrupted by a telephone call, a historic one as it proved.

"Yes, this is the head of the Antifascist Militia speaking. . . . The Italian consul general? . . . You say you have heard that an Italian subject has been arrested and shot by our militia? My dear sir, there must be some mistake; people die in Barcelona but no one is ever shot."

Whatever the facts—and I never learned them—the incident served as a pretext for Mussolini to break off diplomatic relations with the Spanish Republic. The Italian dictator refused to accept the explanation that people were dying in Barcelona only of natural causes. On the strength of his own record he knew something about summary executions.

While obtaining our permits, we were introduced to a Frenchman in the Antifascist Militia. In view of his friendliness we adjourned to a nearby café where, over a drink, we learned something of his background. I shall call him M. to protect his identity, although it is doubtful whether he is still alive. Brought up in Russia as the son of a French consular officer, he had identified himself with the revolutionary movement on its outbreak in 1917 in resentment at his mistreatment at the hands of the czarist police for whistling a revolutionary song, of whose significance he was unaware. He had participated subsequently in the abortive Hungarian and German Communist revolutions. With the failure of the latter he had become a journalist in Paris. Believing that a revolutionary situation was brewing, he had come to Spain in February 1936.

Ehrhard asked him if he was a Communist. "No, I am not. I have never been able to adjust myself to the party's discipline." He paused and added: "You must forgive the expression but, after years of revolutionary activity, I have come to the conclusion that politics is a whore (*la politique, c'est une putain*). Party maneuvering should never obscure the main purpose of our struggle. Life would lose all its meaning for me if the fight in which we are engaged for the freeing of the working class were reduced to nothing more than a fight for power by one faction against another."

As he spoke my mind went back to the Russia I had known in 1921 to 1923. The hopes he was voicing were an echo of those I had heard from men such as Muktarov and Skvartsov. Stalin had ground them under his heel.

In Spain M. had been arrested and imprisoned, and his papers had been seized. Upon his release, with the advent of the Republic, he had recovered most of his belongings except the one possession he prized most, a picture of his mother given him a few days before her death.

M. described for us the defense of Barcelona at which he had
assisted. On the eve of the decisive day, July 17, it was general
knowledge that the army was preparing a *coup d'état*. As the
workers had been denied arms by the Republic, the one means for
the defense of the city was to get into the streets before the military
acted. At dawn on the seventeenth when he saw the working people
swarming out of their homes in answer to an appeal by the Popular
Front, M. told his wife that victory was imminent. The immediate
problem was one of obtaining arms. M. assembled a group of some
forty workers in a truck, and they drove about until they came
upon a military detachment armed with rifles and machine guns.

Then, said M., "we drove toward them with terrific speed, braked
to a stop, and before the troops could recover from their astonishment I yelled to them to abandon their officers and come over to us,
that it would be a crime for them to fire on their own people. Our
fate was hanging by a hair until they responded. It was thus that we
obtained our first arms.

"With reinforcements and arms we moved to an important square
held by the army. When I saw that a body of men had been told off
to attack us, I gave orders for a withdrawal down a side street.
There I ordered half my detachment to take stations in the windows
of the second floor of a building but not to fire until I had given the
signal by a pistol shot. The other half of my men were posted in the
entry ways of adjacent buildings. Waiting until the troops opposing
us had advanced into the street, I took aim at the commander and
fired six shots in rapid succession. There was a fusillade from my
men at the windows which threw the enemy into confusion, while
the other half of my detachment rushed to attack at close range. It
was all over in a few minutes. You have there in miniature the means
by which Barcelona was recovered from the army fascists and the
Republic preserved."

After lunching together at Los Caracoles we went for a walk on
the Ramblas, where M. pointed out a gutted church from whose
belfry he and his men had been fired on in July. "When we entered
the church to seize the offenders I gave strict orders that the priests
should be spared, not suspecting that they had taken part in the
firing. It was only when several had been seized with arms that I
gave order for their execution." He shrugged his shoulders. "They
had only themselves to blame."

Visiting the Department of Agitation and Propaganda, I inquired of the Spaniard in charge if there were any Russians in his organization. I was assured by him, as well as by M., that the only foreigners with the Popular Front in Barcelona were French, German anti-Nazis, and Italian antifascists. When we emerged again on the Ramblas, a procession was forming to do honor to a sixteen-year-old boy who had fallen at the front. There was no music. As the procession got under way, carrying various banners of their organization, the throngs on the street raised their clenched fists in the antifascist salute.

That evening we dined at Los Caracoles in the company of a group of young Frenchmen who had arrived that day from Perpignan with funds for the Spanish Popular Front. They were typical of youths who, in the United States, would have been attending football games; in Europe they had something more serious with which to concern themselves. The evening was passed in a discussion of politics. Now when I go through Perpignan from time to time my mind reverts to those earnest young men, so attractive, so enthusiastic, so full of youthful dreams.

When M. took leave of us that night, he intimated that he was leaving on a dangerous mission with which he had been charged. A few weeks previously he had slipped through Franco's lines with two Spanish companions to sabotage Saragossa's electric and water systems. There was the same lightheartedness and selflessness about him I had remarked in Skvartsov in Russia. Many such were to be found among the revolutionists of those days, but there must be few left today. Stalin took care of most. I think the suspicion must have been forming in M.'s mind that there was something rotten in the state of Denmark when he voiced his conviction that politics was a whore. The successors of Lenin, as well as others in the Western world, were to prove it.

As Ehrhard and I returned by the Ramblas to our hotel, the tramp of many feet could be heard gathering momentum ahead of us in the darkness. We moved to one side with other pedestrians when, out of the night, there loomed like ghosts a body of militiamen with military packs and steel helmets. The majority were mere boys with pinched faces, the older ones with unkempt beards. Someone alongside remarked that they were troops just back from Majorca after an unsuccessful attempt to regain that island for the Republic. There was not a sound as we watched them other than the tramping of their feet and the rustle of the autumn leaves in the trees lining the

Ramblas. The only reaction of the spectators was a raising of clenched fists in greeting; the gesture evoked no response from the troops, worn with fatigue and crushed by their defeat.

Where are they all now? The great majority undoubtedly perished in the initial test of 1936–39 between the forces of democracy and fascism. The tragedy of it was that the lines drawn were far from clear cut. The fascists, represented by Franco, Nazi Germany, and Mussolini's Italy, were on one side of the barricades and, on the other, democratic forces cheek by jowl with totalitarian, Communist Russia. It was the disunity of purpose of those supporting Republican Spain which ensured a Franco victory. I did not see this then, but I did note at the time that the struggle in Spain had a far more than local importance, that it represented a fight "which may still have to be fought, perhaps in France, Great Britain and the United States, unless democracy is to lie down without a struggle before political gangsterism."

We set out the next day for Nice, where Ehrhard left me and I joined my wife at Èze-sur-Mer. From there we headed for Athens to take ship for Egypt, passing by Lake Garda and Riva and thence along the Dalmatian Coast through Spalato, or Split, to Dubrovnik. From the magnificent Gulf of Kotor we began the ascent into Montenegro, through Cetinje, a primitive hamlet. The country was far from reflecting the atmosphere of that Marsovia into which Franz Lehar transformed Montenegro in one of the most delightful of all operettas, *The Merry Widow*. We emerged from the mountains at Peć where seventeen years before Milt Lockwood and I had been given a moving reception as Americans. I had no desire to face our former Yugoslav friends after our failure to realize the hopes that they had expressed so confidently in 1919 of the United States. We pressed on toward Athens and our destination, Egypt.

The Anglo-Egyptian treaty negotiations had temporarily stabilized the Egyptian crisis. It was possible to relax. In consequence we resumed our excursions into the desert, our greatest source of distraction. Once we took ship from Suez to Hurghada, where we drove over a little-traveled route along the Red Sea to Kosseir. From there we headed due west and after surmounting an escarpment of savage grandeur we arrived at the edge of the desert separating us from the Nile. We reduced the air in our tires and, taking care not to waggle the steering wheel, headed west, with no track to guide us, over what appeared to be an endless expanse of sand. Our only compass was the sun. Our main preoccupation was to keep moving as long as we were in sand. At length, after an hour or more, the verdant Nile Valley loomed on the horizon. We made for the nearest village, which was on a main road but twenty miles north of Luxor. There is a fascination in the desert to be found nowhere else in nature—the brooding loneliness, a silence of a spectral character. The loneliness is deeper than that of the sea. In the desert there is no least sound, no echo except possibly in the mind.

From time to time we explored the world's oldest monasteries, those at Wadi Natrun and that at St. Anthony's, reached only by an ill-defined track near the Red Sea. The most interesting was St. Catherine's, a two-day journey by car over the Sinai Peninsula. There the nineteenth-century scholar Konstantin von Tischendorf had found in a waste bin one of the oldest surviving manuscripts of the Bible, which he acquired for a pittance. It passed to the Czar and was later purchased by the British Museum from the Soviet Government. In 1930 Kirsopp Lake of Harvard came with an offer of $10,000 for permission to photograph only the title pages of the manuscript treasures remaining in the monastery. Even the personal intervention of King Fuad did not overcome the obduracy of the ecclesiastical authorities. They had never recovered emotionally from the loss, through ignorance, of their most precious manuscript.

Such was the suspicion aroused by the Lake negotiations, in which I had participated, that when I later visited St. Catherine's I was refused entry into the library. But I had at least some glimpse of the monastery's history when I was shown the refectory, where coats of arms of Crusaders had been carved to commemorate their stay. The outward aspect of the monastery would alone have repaid a visit. Enclosed by ancient walls, it is situated in a small oasis forming the cleft of a narrow valley. The sudden sight of it, after a long journey over the desert and stony hills of Sinai, hidden as a splotch of greenery in an otherwise barren canyon, calls to mind a deceptive mirage.

Egypt itself, with its ancient monuments and the Nile, which threads its way from central Africa to water the crops of a virtually rainless country, the graceful feluccas skimming over its waters and stately palm trees standing along its bank, has something of a mirage-like character. A part of all this, of the desert and of life in Cairo in those days, I sought to put in a novel, half fiction and half fact, entitled *Escape to Cairo*. It fell so flat when published in 1938 that I conceived an aversion for it and could only bring myself to look at it again after twenty years. When I did, I read many passages with incredulity, asking myself, "Was it I who actually wrote these?"

One quotation with a political overtone will suffice, an exchange between a Turkish diplomat and the hero, an American. The time was 1936.

"I admire the English. I spent five years, five very happy years in the Turkish Legation in London. The English are a great race. They have exercised a steadying influence in the world now for several centuries. Like all empires, they have now reached their apogee and are in decline. As the British Empire disintegrates—and the process of disintegration is already to be seen—the same unsettlement of forces will take place as occurred with the decline of the Roman Empire."

"What world force in your view is likely to take its place?"

"Who knows? America might if it were older and more mature. I see no single force capable of taking at this time the place of the British Empire. Perhaps it may represent the last great empire of the world." [3]

This was an epitome of one lesson I had drawn from my five years in Cairo. I had drawn another from my visit to Spain—that the struggle there was a dress rehearsal for one between totalitarianism and human dignity. A third was brought home by what I had seen in Egypt and Spain—that the obtuseness of those in authority was heading us all toward disaster.

VIII

WASHINGTON INTERLUDE

SINCE 1917 I had spent no more than three years in America with the exception of occasional brief months of leave. An assignment early in 1937 to the Near Eastern Division of the Department of State was therefore highly welcome.

As my own state was across the Potomac from Washington, it was unthinkable that we would choose to live anywhere but in Virginia. Under the delusion that we would be able to continue the life we had led in Cairo, where my salary and allowances had permitted us a spacious apartment and three servants, we settled in an eighteenth-century brick house on King Street in Alexandria with a colored cook-maid. At the end of a year we recovered our sense of proportion. By that time my wife was desperate because of the flood of guests our spacious house invited. She found a tiny dwelling, with three rooms and a garden, in a working-class suburb of Alexandria, where we spent the next three years more tranquilly.

There were other even more trying adjustments. At the Department I lost the relative freedom I had enjoyed in Egypt and became a very small cog in a great machine. The work was as impersonal as that in a prison and there were other resemblances. One striking difference was that in a penitentiary there is time off for good behavior; in the Department the initial assignment of three years was extended to a fourth, as mine was, upon satisfactory performance. In the end I came to loathe the work there, so much so that when I was asked to return to Washington in 1945 to a highly responsible post, I declined in the knowledge that I was thereby sacrificing a more promising career than the one I might have in the field. Contentment was by that time more to me than anything else; place and preferment were but empty baubles in comparison.

In the Division of Near Eastern Affairs I had primary responsibility for Palestine, Morocco, Jordan, Egypt, Saudi Arabia, Yemen, Ethiopia, Libya, and Tunisia. Today several officers are occupied with each. I had neither an assistant nor even a secretary; for stenographic aid I drew on the Department's general pool.

However numerous the countries with which I had to deal, there were but two which gave me fairly constant concern, Palestine and Morocco. Happily, the pressure of problems arising in one rarely if ever coincided with pressure in the other. It was the Palestine question which in the beginning made the greatest demands. I had already been made acquainted with its background by my tour of duty in Jerusalem, where I had learned something of the insoluble dilemma imposed on the British by the Balfour Declaration incorporated in the Palestine mandate. From 1925, when I left there, until 1937, when the affairs of that country again became my concern, British policy had oscillated between fulfilling one or the other of the two contradictory provisions of the mandate: one envisaging a National Home for the Jews and the other stipulating that nothing should be done to prejudice the rights of the existing population, an elliptical reference to the Arabs, who constituted the overwhelming majority.

When I assumed my duties in 1937, obtruding with growing persistence was a factor which was to prove controlling in the eventual settlement of the Palestine problem. I refer to the "settlement" eventually reached in the establishment of the state of Israel. The factor in question was the relentless pressure of American Zionists on the British Government, exercised through the American Government, looking to the implementation of the provision of the mandate which favored a Jewish National Home and ignoring the second—safeguarding the rights of the Palestinian Arabs. This Zionist pressure in the end was decisive in dictating both American and British foreign policy toward that country.

It began in 1917 upon the issuance of the Balfour Declaration when Rabbi Stephen Wise obtained from President Wilson his endorsement of the objective of a Jewish National Home in Palestine. No president from Harding to Truman was able to withstand American Zionist pressure for a similar endorsement. There were many American Jews who, far from sharing the goals of the Zionist Organization of America, took sharp issue with them under a conviction that no man can serve two masters. Among them were Rabbi Ephraim Frick and Ambassador Henry Morgenthau, who pointed out that attempts to revive a separate nationality for Jews were a menace to Judaism because they would lead to an ultimate eclipse of

Jewish religious interests by political concerns and would tend "to distract our coreligionists from a full and perfect allegiance to American citizenship and its obligations."

After having permitted massive Jewish immigration which had provoked widespread Arab disorders, British policy, constantly torn between the two conflicting provisions of the mandate, undertook in 1938 to redress the balance. Taking into account the provisions of the mandate safeguarding Arab rights, it was decided to impose a check on Jewish immigration. The reaction of American Zionists was swift and overwhelming. Within a period of one week no less than one hundred thousand letters and telegrams passed over my desk protesting the proposed change in British policy and appealing to the United States Government to intervene. The identical tenor of most of the communications offered clear evidence of the inspired nature of the campaign. There was no attempt at concealment of this on the part of the Zionist Organization of America in its propaganda organ, the *New Palestine* of October 14 and 21, 1938.

In spite of the many voices that were raised to contend that there was no greater American interest involved in this case than there had been when German-Americans protested against our entrance into the war against Germany in 1917 or when Irish-Americans appealed for American intervention with the British Government on behalf of the Irish Republic, the pressure campaign continued. It was undoubtedly the greatest ever brought to bear on the American Government on any foreign issue. For the first time in its history the State Department had to abandon as impracticable individual acknowledgment of the avalanche of communications. Instead a public statement was issued on October 14, 1938, as a collective reply. It reviewed American policy toward Palestine and concluded with the assurance that the Department would "continue to follow the situation closely and will take all necessary measures for the protection of American rights and interests in Palestine."

This carefully weighed statement, drafted at a conference of all members of the Department concerned directly or indirectly with Palestine, in no way responded to Zionist aims. Zionists cared less for vital American interests than for those of their foreign coreligionists. There was, of course, a great humanitarian element in the case, but that called for concerted action by many countries, not action by the United States alone. However understandable their emotions may have been, Zionists could not justify a subordination of American to alien concerns. The result of the statement was renewed pressure, with the bringing up of the Zionist big guns in the form of telegrams from a dozen governors of states and from more than a hundred congressmen, directed both to the President and to the Secretary of State. The former were primarily from areas with a large Jewish population in a position to intimidate irresolute politicians by the threat of withholding votes and party contributions at the command of the Zionist Organization.

In the face of this unexampled pressure Secretary Hull convoked a conference of those officers dealing with the Palestine problem. In the course of it he turned unexpectedly to me to inquire whether I thought there was any possibility that the Arabs in Palestine might be induced to emigrate to neighboring Arab countries to make way for Jews. My reply was that I could not imagine the inducement which could be offered to persuade them to do so.

"Why not?" Mr. Hull shot at me.

I considered for a moment. "Because of the fundamental attachment of every man to his own hearthstone," I answered. I might have placed the question in even more impressive perspective had I, in turn, inquired of Mr. Hull if he could conceive of the white population of his native state of Tennessee relinquishing their lands and homes to make way for an influx of Negroes from neighboring states.

Secretary Hull's questions seemed to me reflective of a politician's viewpoint. To both Mr. Hull and President Roosevelt the issue directly involved the interests of the Democratic party. It was summed up cynically for me by another politician. "Count the votes and you will find the answer. Neither the Democratic nor the Republican party has the slightest interest in the merits of the Palestine problem. There is no Arab vote to speak of in the United States. But consider the number of Zionists in New York, a state which can be crucial in a national election."

The reports in the papers of the unprecedented pressure by American official circles on behalf of Palestine Jews had its inevitable reaction. An Associated Press telegram from Jerusalem on November 1, 1938, reported that

a wave of anti-American sentiment swept Arab communities of the Near East today. This feeling was aroused by the action of a large number of American governors, senators and representatives, and prominent Churchmen, in submitting a memorandum to President Roosevelt urging him to intercede with Great Britain to maintain the Jewish National Home in Palestine and permit undiminished immigration.

A spokesman of the Arab National League in the United States, Dr. Shatars, in appealing for a hands-off policy by the United States, invoked the declaration of President Roosevelt to his fellow countrymen on another subject about that time (November 3, 1938): "Americans have had to put up with a good many things in the course of our history. But the only rule we have ever put up with is the rule of the majority. That is the only rule we will ever put up with."

It was a tragic irony for Arabs that the rule to which American politicians subscribed with passionate devotion elsewhere was not one they were prepared to accept in the case of Palestine. Majority rule was well and good for the United States; it could be urged upon France in North Africa and advocated in behalf of the most primitive peoples of Africa, but it had no application to Palestine.

In an effort to calm Arab bitterness the Department of State instructed its missions in Arab capitals to emphasize that its public statement did not discriminate in any way in favor of Jews to the prejudice of Arabs.

This was the swan song of the State Department in the exercise of effective influence in the shaping of American foreign policy on Palestine. From that time on—from 1938 to 1953—anything having to do with the formulation, however indirect, of policy passed progressively out of the hands of professional career officers, whose sole concern was the protection of American interests, and was dictated more and more exclusively by the White House in the light of domestic political considerations. Secretary James Forrestal recounts in his *Diaries* his unsuccessful efforts with leaders of both parties to take the issue out of politics so that it might be dealt with solely on the basis of the foreign interests of the United States.

The Department's efforts to stem the tide of anti-American feeling on the part of the Arabs were soon compromised by domestic developments. Responding to the intervention of his Zionist constituents, Senator Robert Wagner of New York called on the President on October 23 and on emerging from the White House issued a statement that the President

was prepared to take more than normal action, that he and the United States Government were in favor of the maintenance of Palestine as the Jewish National Home without limitation, that he was watching the situation closely and that he would do everything in the power of the Government to prevent the curtailment of [Jewish] immigration. This statement did nothing to diminish Arab outbursts against the United States.

With the advent of 1939 and the growing menace of Hitler Germany, pressure by the White House on the British Government in behalf of Zionists was momentarily relaxed. For a brief period the exigencies of American domestic politics were subordinated to the necessity of dealing with the German threat against the security of the Western world. In consequence, greater attention had to be paid to the appeasement of the Arabs by the tempering of measures antagonistic to them. In the light of these circumstances the British Government, after vainly seeking in a conference called in London between Arabs and Jews to work out the basis of an agreement on the future of Palestine, issued a declaration on May 17, 1939, unilaterally fixing its policy. An independent Palestine state, possibly of a federal nature, was to be established within ten years. Jewish immigration was to be permitted until the Jewish proportion of the population had risen from the existing ratio of 28 per cent to one-third. It was observed that the framers of the Palestine mandate "could never have intended that Palestine should be converted into a Jewish State against the will of the Arab population of the country."

Such an admission seemed incontrovertible except to Zionist extremists. In a call which the future president of Israel, Dr. Chaim Weizmann, made on the chief of the Division of Near Eastern Affairs in the Department of State on February 6, 1940, he remarked with some plaintiveness that "American Zionists were either uncompromising in their outlook or completely disillusioned regarding the future." [1]

With the advent of war the British declaration of May 17, 1939, was pushed into the background. It was challenged later and rendered nugatory in the emotional atmosphere engendered by Hitler's inhuman treatment of the Jews. By one of the ironies of history it may well be that Hitler's most permanent memorial will be the state of Israel. It is inconceivable that any circumstance other than a guilt complex over a callous failure to react in time to Hitler's Jewish policy could have so blinded the world to the subsequent injustice in forcing more than a million Arabs to provide *Lebensraum* for Jews in Palestine. This was the supreme tragedy, the world's failure to raise a hand in 1931 to stay Hitler's initial measures against the Jews. There was, however, no reason in equity or justice that the United States should have called upon the Arabs, who had no responsibility for the inception of the problem, to carry the entire burden of its solution. It was certainly no part of the viewpoint exposed by Dr. Weizmann when he reviewed the Palestine problem in 1940 with us in the Department of State.

The strain put on me by Palestine and the many other recurring problems of my work resulted in the appearance late in 1938 of a duodenal ulcer, which confined me for forty-two days in the Naval Hospital. It was a product perhaps less of work than worry. In 1939 at the age of forty-six my income was no more than it had been twenty years earlier. In sixteen years I had advanced three grades in the service.

With Palestine temporarily out of the way, Morocco became a problem. With the relinquishment of our extraterritorial rights in Egypt in 1937 by the Montreux Convention of that year, the French Government had approached us with the project of a treaty looking to the same end in Morocco. Leon Marchal, of the French protectorate administration, came to Washington to work out with us the provisions of such a treaty. After some weeks in the sweltering heat of the summer of 1939 and with the aid of Harry Turkel of the Legal Division, we came to an agreement on all but two points. Marchal returned to Paris and Rabat to seek higher advice about these, and it was decided that I would join him later in Morocco to investigate on the spot their practical significance for us.

The day I sailed for Cherbourg the Soviet-German Pact was announced. If there had been knowledge of it one day earlier, my mission would have been canceled as purposeless, for, with the pact's signature, it was clear that Hitler was on the point of striking. On the station platform in Paris I found awaiting me an old friend of Bucharest days, Henri de Malval, who had read of my scheduled arrival in the press. We dined at Ramponneau's, and over our meal he debated whether or not to leave his most precious family possessions in his flat in Paris or move them for safekeeping to his chateau. The next day he transported what he could in his car to his country home with the result that they were lost when pillaged a few months later by his own fellow countrymen, while his apartment remained untouched during the German occupation. We went on to the Bal Tabarin, which was filled with merrymakers who gave no evidence of any concern about a Second World War, the curtain on which was to rise in a matter of hours.

Two days later, with the announcement of French mobilization, I boarded a train for Marseilles. From Gibraltar I reached Tangier by British ferry and from there Rabat. With the outbreak of war all thoughts of a treaty were temporarily put aside. There was nothing to do but return to the United States by the nearest available transport, a freighter of the American Export Line from Casablanca. My visit was not, however, without some useful purpose in making known to me at firsthand a country with which I was to be intimately concerned for some years.

Soon after my return to Washington I was confronted with a problem arising from the President's unfamiliarity with some of the less simple elements of foreign affairs. It was occasioned by the appointment of Myron Taylor as the President's special representative to the Vatican, an appointment which had aroused a furor in Protestant circles. As a means of neutralizing this, Roosevelt conceived the notion of naming similar special representatives to the principal religious faiths in the Near East. I first heard of it when Wallace Murray showed me a memorandum from Adolph Berle, enclosing a request from the President for a list of such leaders.

I regarded Wallace incredulously when he asked for my reaction. "It's absolutely cockeyed," I said. "Since the abolition of the caliphate there has been no head of the Islamic world except for a fleeting assertion of the title by King Hussein, who lost his throne as a result. The King of Egypt aspires to it but even the King of Saudi Arabia, who is in possession of the Holy Places, one of the essential attributes of a caliph, refuses to arrogate that title to himself. Then there are the two great sects of Islam, the Sunnis and the Shi'as. There is today no spiritual head of either; since the abolition of the caliphate every Moslem sovereign has assumed spiritual as well as temporal leadership over his subjects. As far as Christian faiths in the Near East are concerned, the Orthodox Church is a state establishment. You can see the complications."

Wallace agreed and instructed me to prepare a memorandum for Berle along those lines. A few days later he informed me that on its receipt the President had remarked with some heat that he had not asked the State Department for reasons why his proposal was impractical but for means for its implementation. Wallace agreed that, other than the duplication of our diplomatic missions, none were available if we did not wish to stir up a dozen hornets' nests in naming representatives to spiritual heads of our arbitrary choice. He suggested that I attack the question with more vigor for a *reductio ad absurdum* of the idea. I did so and that was the last we heard of it.

Roosevelt was a consummate war leader and generally farsighted in dealing with purely domestic problems. In foreign affairs, in the conduct of which, with mistaken conceit, he prided himself, he all too often showed himself a tyro. The tragedy was that the President made no effective use of the State Department, the agency charged with conducting foreign affairs. Cordell Hull was Secretary of State in name only. The Department was, of course, permitted to transact ordinary routine business. Questions of high policy, however, were not only taken out of its hands but they were not even referred for comment and advice to the professional civil servants in the Department who had given a lifetime to the study of foreign affairs. It is normal constitutional practice for a president to determine the ultimate direction of foreign policy, but a disregard of the State Department amounting to almost contempt for its experts distinguished President Roosevelt from both his predecessors and his successors.

Behind this was the prejudice of the President against the foreign service. He had grown up with many idle sons of the rich who had entered the diplomatic service when wealth was essential for admittance to it. Before the passage of the Rogers Act of 1924 the top post in the diplomatic service, that of counselor, an officer second only to an ambassador, drew a maximum salary of $3,000, as compared with $12,000 for a consul general. The Rogers Act amalgamated the diplomatic and consular services with a uniform scale of salaries, making competence rather than the possession of private means the test of a candidate for the diplomatic branch, but Roosevelt's unfavorable estimate of the foreign service had been formed before the act was enacted. There can be no disputing that his judgment of it, on the basis of the knowledge he had gained prior to 1924, was more than justified. Since 1924, however, the service had been transformed. By 1930, with major amputations effected by the removal of the deadwood which had encumbered it in the persons of playboys who used it for their social advancement and amusement, it was one worthy of the United States. It was too late, however, to bring about any alteration of the President's prejudice.

As Assistant Secretary of the Navy under Wilson, Roosevelt had been thrown in intimate contact with the officers of the armed services. After entering the White House in 1933, it was to many of these old friends such as Admiral William D. Leahy and General Pat Hurley, along with such outsiders as William C. Bullitt, that he turned for advice on policy matters in foreign affairs.

With the fall of France in 1940 and the conclusion of an armistice with Germany on June 22, French North Africa overnight assumed extraordinary strategic importance for both the Allies and the United States. In the belief that Britain's surrender was only a matter of weeks Hitler had left this area, including Morocco, Tunisia, and Algeria, free of any control other than that of a small armistice commission. Under the State Department's geographical distribution of territories, Morocco and Tunisia were responsibilities of the Near Eastern Affairs Division, but Algeria, as an integral part of France, fell under the European Division, an anomaly which was to play a significant role subsequently in the execution of American policy in that area.

As early as July 1939 I had prepared for Secretary Hull an analysis of some of the strategic and political developments likely to arise in the Mediterranean area from a Second World War. In that study I concluded that Spain would probably remain neutral, that France was capable of defending its North African possessions, and that the Allies were in a position to retain command of Gibraltar and the Dardanelles, as well as the Suez Canal. My final conclusion was that Great Britain and France apparently had the means to hold their own generally in the Mediterranean and in North Africa and, with time, reduce Italy, if it became a belligerent, by economic pressure if through no other means.

With my attention thus focused on the Mediterranean and, in particular, on French North Africa, the arrival of General Maxime Weygand in Algiers on October 9, 1940, as French proconsul of that area, attracted my immediate notice. It led me to mull over the significance of his presence and how we might profit from the special status of French North Africa following the French capitulation. I began to examine the means by which this strategic area might be preserved from German domination. The idea naturally followed that such an end would be best attained through the extension of economic aid.

In a 16-page memorandum entitled "The Political Implications of American-Moroccan Trade" I concluded:

From our larger defense interests it is important that French Morocco should not fall into hostile hands, and anything done to bolster the morale of the authorities and people of that area and to avoid the collapse, whether economic or political of French Morocco would appear to be in our interest.[2]

Shortly after starting work on the study I had an unexpected call in my office on October 25 of an old Near Eastern acquaintance, Arthur Reed, Socony-Vacuum representative in Morocco. He could not have confirmed more strikingly the validity of the memorandum's thesis. Reed disclosed that one of the principal preoccupations of General Auguste Noguès, French Resident General at Rabat, was to prevent Morocco from being overrun by the Germans. His subordinate, Emmanuel Monick, had conceived as a means to that end relaxation of the British blockade to permit trade with us. To solicit British agreement Leon Marchal had been sent from Rabat to Madrid to confer secretly with David Eccles, head of British Economic Warfare for the Iberian Peninsula at the British Embassy in Spain, and Reed had been charged by Monick, with Noguès' approval, to proceed to Washington to explore the ground. Reed confirmed the conclusion I had hazarded in my memorandum that Weygand had been sent to Algiers by Petain to safeguard the French position in North Africa and to keep it out the Axis orbit.[3]

Further confirmation of the validity of my thesis came in a telegram of November 6 from our embassy in Vichy reporting a call from Monick. He had emphasized the great importance attached to American-Moroccan trade and had declared that both Weygand and Noguès were determined not to accept any German foothold in Morocco.

As encouragement to Monick I drafted a reply, which went out under Secretary Hull's signature on November 9, instructing our Vichy embassy to inform Monick that consideration was being given to the possibility of arriving at some arrangement taking into account the views he had expressed. This was the first official action of the American Government looking to an economic accord on the subject of French North Africa.

With the completion of my memorandum Wallace Murray and I conferred with Assistant Secretary of State Berle on how best to achieve its practical application. As a first step to that end it was agreed that I should draft telegrams to our representatives in Algiers and Tangier to make known to Generals Weygand and Noguès our willingness to cooperate through economic measures with the French in North and West Africa.

Thus was born the conception which found realization a few months later, in February 1941, in the Weygand-Murphy Accord. As worked out by General Weygand and Robert Murphy, it provided for commercial exchange of goods between the United States and French North Africa under the supervision of specially appointed vice consuls, nominally attached to the consulates at Casablanca, Algiers, and Tunis but responsible directly to Murphy in Algiers. These special agents, along with the State Department's regularly appointed foreign service officers in that area and a host of assistants delegated to them, prepared the ground for the Allied landings in French North Africa in November 1942.

Between the dispatch of the two telegrams and the consummation of the accord many obstacles had to be overcome. Strangely enough, the telegrams themselves were held for some days on the desk of Dr. Herbert Feis, economic adviser to the Department, who was so opposed to the policy that they were ultimately sent out only over his protest. Even after the accord was reached, the Treasury Department, which had supervision over the issuance of export permits and was as concerned as Feis that the agreement might eventually play into German hands, resorted to every possible dilatory tactic.

Other cross-currents were at work. At the end of November we learned that realization of this economic aid accord born in the Near Eastern Division was to be taken not only out of our hands but out of those of the Department as well. Bullitt, former Ambassador to France, to whom the President gave greater ear in foreign affairs than to his Secretary of State, had proposed that negotiation of the accord be entrusted to one of his protégés, Robert Murphy, answerable directly to the White House.

As Murphy was then serving as counselor of embassy at Vichy, he could be detached from that post and assigned with the same rank to the consulate general at Algiers, then a part of Metropolitan France, without altering his situation vis-à-vis the French. In Algiers his jurisdiction officially extended only over Algeria, but unofficially he was charged with supervision over the special vice consuls assigned to all three consulates in French North Africa, namely, at Algiers, Tunis, and Casablanca.

That Murphy had been specifically instructed by the White House to ignore the Department of State in his mission to Algiers was made evident when he failed to confer with Wallace Murray, at the latter's express invitation, on the measures taken by us to obtain the economic accord which he had been charged to negotiate with Weygand. Although lacking experience in North African problems, Murphy was possessed of indubitable charm. Indeed, his sparkling personality and lightness of touch may in themselves have been handicaps in the subsequent execution of his exceptionally delicate task.

Late in 1939 I was informed that, with the transfer of the American diplomatic agent who headed the legation in Tangier, I was to take it over as chargé d'affaires *a.i.* upon the expiration of my four years of duty in the Department. I had no intimation that I would be left there for almost five years. When, at the end of two or three years, I was asked by the curious what "a.i." meant, I replied that officially it stood for *ad interim* but that I was beginning to suspect that it actually represented, in my particular case, *ad infinitum*. As head of the legation I would be directly responsible for American interests in the Tangier, Spanish, and French zones of Morocco.

IX

MOROCCO AND THE NORTH AFRICAN ALLIED LANDINGS[1]

M Y NEW post was one normally held by an officer of the highest grade. As I was in Class IV, I was considerably short of it. The post was to bring with it my crowded hour: within the brief space of three years I passed to Class III in 1942, to II in 1944, and to I in 1945.

To reach Tangier I took ship with my wife for Lisbon and motored from there to Algeciras. Spain was so close to starvation after three years of civil strife that we were obliged to supplement the food both at the Hotel d'Angleterre in Seville and at the elegant Maria Christina in Algeciras with provisions foresightedly carried with us. In the first telegram I sent from Tangier I reported that Spain, on the threshold of starvation, was not in a position to enter the war and that if it did it would prove a most ineffective partner of Hitler. A like opinion was shortly to be expressed by Spanish officials in Tangier.

I assumed charge of the legation on February 3, 1941, and I remained there until June 1945. It was one of our most picturesque foreign service establishments, situated in the heart of the native city and with no access to it except by foot. The original building and grounds, considerably extended since then, had been a gift to our government about 1820 from the Sultan. President Roosevelt referred to it in a letter to the reigning Sultan at the time of the American landings as one made to George Washington, who, in 1820, had long been in his grave.

France had been granted a protectorate over Morocco in 1912, Spain a subprotectorate over a strip in the north, while in 1923 an international regime had been formed for the administration of an enclave around Tangier, commanding the strategic Straits of Gibraltar. With our recognition in 1917 of the French protectorate we formally assumed an obligation to deal exclusively in all matters relating to Morocco with the French Resident General as the Sultan's Minister for Foreign Affairs. This was ignored, to the understandable irritation of the French, when President Roosevelt at the Casablanca Conference in 1943 conferred privately with the Sultan.

We had never recognized the Spanish Zone, where a Spanish High Commissioner had his seat at Tetuán. Nor had we recognized, even *de facto* as did other powers, Spanish occupation on November 3, 1940, of the Tangier Zone, when, with the collapse of France, the international administration had been unilaterally dissolved and a Spanish Administrator appointed responsible to the High Commissioner in Tetuán.

Our nonrecognition of the Spanish Zone, including that of Tangier, coupled with Spain's close ties with the Axis, rendered the position of the American Legation at Tangier when I took over an exceedingly delicate one vis-à-vis the Spanish. It was obvious that they could not be ignored if I were effectively to discharge my duties to keep the Department of State informed both of Spanish and French intentions in Morocco in that critical period. It was not to be accomplished by withdrawing into lofty isolation.

The knowledge gained of Spain on my visit to Barcelona in 1936 had not favorably disposed me toward the Franco regime. My own personal convictions, however, could play no part in the execution of my official mission. My duty was clear: I had to cultivate the Spanish if I were to gain knowledge of their purposes. In common with many I was convinced that the Spanish Government was fascist and totalitarian and that its destinies were bound up with the Axis. I was right in the first assumption but in error on the second. As I discovered, the Spaniard is first, last, and always a Spaniard, with no attachment, sentimental or otherwise, to any country but his own. If at the beginning of the war Spain identified itself with the Axis in a nonbelligerent status, it was the better to serve Spanish interests. As Axis pressure relaxed and Allied fortunes rose, Spain moved toward closer association with the latter. Cynical, yes, but a reflection of *realpolitik* and responsive to Spanish needs.

After a Moorish domination of seven centuries, the Spaniard is a mixture of Arab and Latin. From the former he has acquired a profound sense of personal dignity, honor, and *noblesse oblige*. He resembles the Arab in his impatience with legal abracadabra. Confidence, cultivated by personal contact, is everything; appeal to abstract principles, mumbo jumbo to him. Spanish officials, as later

Arabs in Arabia were often to remark to me: "Don't bother to write. Come and let us talk it over and settle everything without formality."

My first overtures to the Spanish were not encouraging. In an informal call on the Spanish Administrator of Tangier, an army officer, I was not even proffered a seat. Mindful that the breaking of bread with an Arab may turn an enemy into a friend, I subsequently invited the Administrator to lunch and thereby won the second round. The cultivation of General Luis Orgaz, High Commissioner, got off to a less propitious start. When I failed to attend a function honoring the assumption of his new duties, he took his grievances against me to Sir Samuel Hoare, British Ambassador in Madrid, who made them known to his American colleague, Alexander Weddell. The latter assured Hoare that, as I was an officer of some experience, he could not believe my action had been dictated by caprice.[2] Upon Orgaz' return to Tetuán I called on him unofficially and explained to his satisfaction that I had only been conforming with the instructions of my government. I assured him that my absence from Spanish official functions in view of our nonrecognition of the Spanish position in Morocco was not to be interpreted as any lack of desire on my part to place our relations informally on the most friendly possible basis.

Orgaz, who had been Captain General of Catalonia, was a man of few words with the traditional gruffness of a soldier and the reputation among his own people of a tartar. Early in our acquaintance I sized him up as at heart a sentimentalist. At my next interview I laid siege to him with an admiring reference to the important Spanish contributions to American civilization. His eyes brightened. The Spanish, he said, had many shortcomings but they were a romantic and generous people. I ultimately gained both his confidence and friendship.

The insight I acquired into his character was to be put to effective use. A year later, in a call on him with our petroleum attaché from Madrid, Walter Smith, we were on the point of leaving after Orgaz had given Smith a severe going-over, when I asked Walter to interpret in his fluent Spanish my request that we be permitted to open a consulate in Ceuta. It was an observation post of some importance to us if we were to effect landings in French North Africa. Walter objected that the High Commissioner was in too vile a mood to be receptive. I insisted and was amused by the expression on Smith's face as Orgaz beamingly agreed.

A year or more later I had a call from Mme Renée Reichmann, a Jewish refugee, who after her arrival had interested herself in welfare activities affecting her coreligionists. On the basis of the influence I was known to enjoy with Orgaz she solicited my intervention with him to approve issuance by the Spanish Legation in Budapest of Spanish Moroccan visas for five hundred Jewish children threatened with extermination. The granting of the visas would not necessitate their physical transfer to Morocco but would ensure their escape from the Axis incinerators.

Although the action she proposed was wholly outside my sphere and competence, I could not remain deaf to her appeal. When I presented it to Orgaz, he gave his accord without hesitation. When Mme Reichmann called to express her appreciation, she asked, in view of the success attending the initial approach, that perhaps I might be disposed to renew it in behalf of another seven hundred children. I saw Orgaz again and again he agreed. A few days before my final departure from Tangier I had a letter from Mme Reichmann in which she wrote:

The International Red Cross in Budapest were able, thanks to the entry visas for Tangier, to obtain the release of 1,200 Jews from a Nazi concentration camp, put them in safety in a house rented for the purpose, which, through the authorization given for visas, was protected by the Spanish Consulate in Budapest. Thus, 1,200 innocent souls owe their having been saved to Your Excellency.

Even though Mme Reichmann credited me, who had served only as an intermediary, with a humanitarian result properly belonging to her in the first instance and to Orgaz in the last, the testimony was gratifying.

Face plays so great a part in the Near East that upon my arrival in Tangier I had been disturbed by failure of the Sultan's representative, the Mendoub, to return my official call. It was of all the greater concern because I was aware that I was under scrutiny for the detection of any weakness in the exercise of my duties. I instructed the legation dragoman to call on the Mendoub and express my regrets at his indisposition. He departed, shaking his head, but he returned smiling broadly to inform me that the Sultan's representative had been at first as puzzled as he by the message. " 'But, Mr.

Abrines, I am not sick,' he said. 'That is what I told the chargé.' Then his face broke into a grin. 'I begin to understand. Tell him I shall call at the legation tomorrow at three.' " I had resolved the contretemps in a manner to which the Mendoub could not take exception. There is nothing an Arab is fonder of than a battle of wits, particularly one in which the vanquished is not made to lose face but may yield gracefully and laugh when outdone. I had not immersed myself for years in the seventeen volumes of the *Thousand and One Nights* for nothing.

The official business which I had to transact concerning French Morocco was conducted with General Auguste Noguès, French Resident General at Rabat, five hours by car from Tangier. From the time of my arrival until the American landings during the night of November 7, 1942, I enjoyed the most cordial relations with the Resident and his staff. This friendly atmosphere was attributable not only to the Weygand-Murphy Economic Accord of February 26, 1941, but equally to the profoundly anti-Axis sentiment of the overwhelming majority of the French in North Africa.

Noguès was one of the most outstanding officers in the French Army. For a moment, in June 1940, it appeared that he might assume the leadership of those French elements outside Metropolitan France who were considering disassociating themselves from Vichy following the conclusion of an armistice with Germany. The hesitation of the French authorities in Syria and Lebanon in responding to his soundings, together with that traditional French attachment to the principle of legality, were considerations which eventually persuaded him to bow before what seemed inexorable events. Trained in the traditions of the proconsulship in Morocco of Marshal Louis Lyautey, Noguès had acquired so strong a position during his own that he had kept his post during the many political changes in France since he assumed his duties in 1936.

Slim and wiry, of medium height, with a dry manner characteristic of many French, I found him most favorably disposed to the Allied cause and particularly to the United States. His paramount loyalty was understandably to France. His overriding passion was the unimpaired maintenance of France's tie with Morocco. His conspicuous success could not have been more strikingly evidenced than in the ability he displayed in this regard during the lowest ebb in French fortunes and despite the presence in Morocco of a German armistice commission from the collapse of France in 1940 to the

The Spanish Moroccan guard of honor at the Spanish-French Moroccan frontier on the occasion of General George Patton's visit to General Luis Orgaz

The Khalifa at Tetuán, Spanish Morocco, in 1944

Allied landings in November 1942. When I expressed admiration of the firmness he had shown in forbidding any contact on the part of that commission with either French or Moroccans except in execution of the commission's official functions, his reply was: "I had to show the Germans that it is we who are still masters in Morocco." He did so with great effectiveness. I was privileged to gain his confidence early and was taken into the intimacy of his home—an exceptional mark of friendliness on the part of a Frenchman—lunching on occasions privately with him and Mme Noguès, daughter of the famous Prime Minister Théophile Delcassé. Emmanuel Monick, Jacques Meyrier, Roger du Gardier, Bernard Hardion, and Pierre Charpentier, Noguès' principal assistants, were as cordial and as helpful to me as their chief.

I was particularly fortunate in finding as French consul in Tetuán Claude Clarac, whom I had known seven years earlier in Persia. The position he occupied in so strategic an area enabled him to pass me information of considerable importance to the Allies. My greatest difficulty was in convincing him that he was far more valuable both to his country as well as to our common effort in remaining as Vichy representative rather than resigning and joining de Gaulle in London. It was a constant battle on my part with him. When the landings no longer made his presence at Tetuán important, he resigned his post to join de Gaulle, who subsequently appointed him ambassador.

Of the many pressing problems facing us, one of prime importance was whether the Spanish, taking advantage of French weakness, might he tempted to extend their influence in Morocco. An authoritative outline of the official Spanish attitude was given me as early as May 12, 1941, by my Spanish colleague. He assured me of general opposition to Spanish entry into the war. The Germans were much too preoccupied with the eastern Mediterranean to concern themselves simultaneously with the western part. About the same time Colonel Juan Beigbeder, former Spanish Foreign Minister, on a visit to Tetuán informed me by private confidential message of a meeting of Spanish generals who had recorded their unanimous opposition to Spanish participation in the war or the granting of permission to German forces to traverse Spain.

While these were reassuring indexes, it would have been folly to rely on them alone. I proposed to Washington that we bind Spanish Morocco to us through an economic accord similar to that negotiated with the French. The Department of State looked favorably upon the suggestion, but not so the Spanish authorities, still apprehensive of Axis reaction. I then proposed that we exercise economic pressure to demonstrate to the Spanish on which side their bread was buttered by withholding vital supplies such as petroleum products and rubber tires, of which we were then their sole supplier.

Difficulties encountered by the Germans in their invasion of Russia in June 1941 induced Spain to be less impressed by supposed German invincibility. In the meanwhile the Spanish Zone was beginning to feel the pinch of the economic measures we had introduced. With our entrance into the war in December, Clarac informed me the next month that he had reason to believe Orgaz was disposed to adopt a more independent line in Spanish Morocco and, with a view to preserving the *status quo* in the western Mediterranean, to work in close concert with French Morocco and Portugal.

The report of these developments to Washington had immediate repercussions. At the end of January 1942 I had an important addition to my staff in the person of Colonel William A. Eddy, assigned as naval attaché and charged also with the direction of all American intelligence activities in French North Africa. Eddy brought with him a message from the Department authorizing me, in my discretion, to make overtures to Orgaz to assure him of the moral and material support of the United States in the event of any attempt by the Axis to involve Spain and Spanish Morocco in war.

Since Eddy's departure from Washington, however, the tide of war had taken a lightning turn in North Africa with a drive by Rommel which threatened Egypt. The time was clearly inopportune for an approach to Orgaz. In March, with another shift, on this occasion favorable to the Allies, I cautiously sounded out Orgaz along the lines of the authority given me. When the High Commissioner announced categorically that it was inconceivable that Spain would ever take up arms against us, I pursued the opening by proposing an economic accord. Shortly thereafter we negotiated a limited one affecting petroleum products under the supervision of an attaché assigned for that purpose to the legation.[3] Within a little more than twelve months we had succeeded in transforming a hardly concealed hostility toward us into close mutual confidence. It was to serve us in good stead on the night of November 7, 1942, when Vice Admiral H. K. Hewitt flung his Western Task Force on the Moroccan beaches.

As a gateway to North Africa under neutral control, Tangier since 1940 had become an important center of both Allied and Axis espionage and counterespionage activities. Sabotage was one of the common weapons, so much so that I never failed to have my car inspected before I entered it to detect the possible presence of a bomb. On January 12, 1942, a British sabotage unit blew up with dynamite charges a radio station in the city through which the Axis was communicating with German submarines in the Straits. In retaliation the Germans placed a bomb in a taxicab, stationed at the docks, timed to explode with the arrival by ferry of a British courier. The king's messenger was killed along with a number of other innocent bystanders.

I was kept closely acquainted with these activities by the British even before our entrance into the war. In consonance with our government's policy toward the Allies I had taken the initiative in instituting a Joint Anglo-American Intelligence Committee, which was of far more profit to the British than to us, lacking as they did official representation in French North Africa. The only serious dispute I ever had with my British colleague was when he sought to have transmitted through our diplomatic bag to Casablanca explosive materials destined for one of Murphy's vice consuls for the destruction of rubber in transit for Germany. I objected that the rubber was of less importance than the possible compromising of our special agents operating under the economic accord. "I suppose you are aware," he observed, "that the British Government has means of dealing with American diplomats who are lukewarm in aiding our war effort. A word from the Foreign Office to the State Department might not make your position too comfortable." I suggested that he had overlooked the fact that I was an officer of the American and not of the British Government.

After the arrival of Eddy all undercover transactions of the legation were left to his supervision. His most spectacular achievement was the smuggling out of Morocco of Malvergne, chief French pilot at Port Lyautey, to guide the Western Task Force into Moroccan waters in November 1942. Two of Eddy's assistants proceeded to Port Lyautey and under cover of darkness transported the pilot in a car to Tangier. Before crossing from the French into the Spanish Zone the pilot was concealed in a trailer covered with a tarpaulin. Every possible mishap had been foreseen but one, the barking of a dog, attracted by the pilot's scent when the trailer stopped for passport inspection at the frontier. Happily, the frontier officials were inside their offices and were not alerted by the barking, to which an end was speedily put by a rock deftly thrown by one of the Americans.

The first intimation of Operation Torch, the code name by which the contemplated Allied landings in French Morocco were designated, came to me through the June 1942 visit of Colonel Robert Solborg, Military Attaché in Lisbon. Upon his arrival he disclosed in great confidence a directive from the Joint Chiefs of Staff authorizing him to sound out the situation with view to determining the French officer offering the greatest appeal as a soldier in rallying French forces of French North Africa at the time of our projected landings.

From Tangier we drove to Rabat, where I introduced him to a French officer known to be most favorably disposed to the Allies, Colonel Koeglin-Schwarz, who could be approached with less formality than General Noguès. We met the former clandestinely, and Solborg, in discreet questions without disclosing the object of his mission, drew from the colonel the opinion that Henri Giraud was the officer to whom the French Army in North Africa would most readily respond in an emergency. As we emerged, Solborg remarked that the viewpoint advanced was also held strongly by many others, including Jacques Lemaigre-Debreuil, with whom he had an appointment the following day in Casablanca. Some ten days later Solborg reappeared in Tangier. He had met his French coconspirator Lemaigre-Debreuil, who had gone thereafter to France to sound out Giraud. Upon the former's return to Algiers he had acquainted Solborg and Murphy of the willingness of Giraud to put himself at the head of those French forces who might associate themselves with the Allies.

Colonel Eddy returned on September 5, 1942, from consultations in Washington to inform me that plans for the landings had so far advanced that their time had been fixed for late October or early November. Their imminence would be apparent in the passage through the Straits of immense convoys as well as by his own departure for Gibraltar to join General Eisenhower's staff. I had earlier expressed to Solborg, as I did again to Eddy, apprehension over our ability to keep concealed from the Axis a project conceived so many months in advance. That we were successful in this respect has always seemed to me something of a miracle.[4]

The maintenance of the confidential character of the operation was all the more remarkable in that, as we learned afterward, the German intelligence service had been able to place one of its agents in our legation. In the summer of 1942 friendly French intelligence sources informed our naval attaché that they had intercepted and read a German code message from the German consulate in Tangier to Berlin quoting a message we had sent to Tunis on behalf of our naval attaché. Persistent efforts to discover how the leak had occurred proved fruitless. On most insubstantial evidence the assistant naval attaché reported to Washington that the German agent was a woman employee in our chancery. I was instructed to dismiss her. Persuaded of her innocence I resisted, with the result that the order to me was rescinded.

It was months later that the mystery was solved by chance. A Spaniard who had been invited to work for the Office of Strategic Services disclosed that he was already working for the Germans. He would have preferred to work for us but for the presence of a German agent in our midst. The sum of money offered him was sufficient to loosen his tongue. The German agent proved to be a Spanish charwoman in the office of our naval attaché. She had been given a master key capable of unlocking any file cabinet, as well as a special camera for the photographing of documents.

On the eve of the landings two questions absorbed us: the possible reaction of Spain and Spanish Morocco on the one hand and that of the French protectorate authorities on the other. I had expressed the view to Washington as early as September 1, 1942, that our landings would be likely to provoke renewed Axis demands on Spain but that the Spanish would make every effort to avoid any commitments. On Sunday morning November 8 as the landings were in progress I headed for Tetuán in my car to gain all possible knowledge of Spanish intentions in the light of the unexpected appearance of our armed forces. They had so far caught the Spanish unawares that the High Commissioner was absent in Madrid. From his next in command, General Salvador Múgica, I was able to form a clear impression which I telegraphed to the State Department a few hours later: "The Spanish will not stir from the Spanish Zone." [5]

The probable reaction of the French protectorate authorities was, of course, of far more crucial importance and one which I had been at pains to present to the Department over a period of more than a year. The initial armed resistance which our forces encountered in

French North Africa came as a great shock both to the American public and to General Eisenhower. It was less of a shock, however, to the American Legation in Tangier.

As early as June 9, 1941, General Noguès had expressed to me in the most categoric terms his intention to defend French Morocco against an attack "from any source." Reiterating this to me on November 30, 1941, he expressed the view that it was in our mutual interest for Morocco not to be drawn into the conflict, adding that he would take every measure available to him to defend it if menaced from any quarter. On June 5, 1942, Noguès again defined his position unequivocally. At that time he stated to me: "Morocco is very favorably disposed to the United States, but we shall resist any effort to attack us by whomever it is made, and I hope you will emphasize this to your government." He added the opinion that nothing would draw the Germans to North Africa quicker than a belief that an Anglo-American operation was impending there.[6] These statements outlining his position were telegraphed to Washington, of course. Fortunately the Germans never credited us with the ability to launch such an operation. Unfortunately Noguès shared this skepticism.

The warnings we continued to give from Tangier were many. On August 18, 1942, I telegraphed an expression of Clarac's opinion that Noguès would defend Morocco. Ten days before the landings I quoted the statement to me by a high official of the French consulate in Tangier that unless an Allied landing coincided with a political crisis in France it would meet with determined resistance.

In order to appreciate Noguès' reaction let us endeavor to place ourselves in his position when confronted with the actual operation. He had no notion nor any least intimation from us that it was within the capacity of the Allies to undertake a major military operation in French North Africa. There was nothing he feared more than an Allied landing in insufficient strength, which would instantly provoke German counter measures. His dominant purpose was to preserve Morocco intact. That his fears were not exaggerated was to be proved by subsequent events in Tunisia.

Had we adopted the measures available to us to convince Noguès that our landings would be made in sufficient strength to ensure their success, he would not have moved unless to offer a purely token resistance to fulfill the obligations he conceived due to Marshal Pétain as chief of state. We not only failed to take such measures but, what was equally lamentable, the means which were taken to notify him of our intentions on the night of the landings could not possibly have been more ineptly conceived.

It was known or should have been known in Washington by the character of the reports the legation in Tangier had been making for months preceding the landings that I enjoyed the particular confidence of General Noguès. It was certainly known to the American military authorities. I was present when a declaration to this effect was made in June 1942 by du Gardier, the chief of Noguès' diplomatic cabinet, to the newly arrived American military attaché of the legation. On that occasion the French diplomat affirmed to the military attaché that the chargé d'affaires of the legation in Tangier enjoyed the confidence of the Resident General as no other American known to him. Yet the legation at Tangier, charged with the responsibility for American interests in Morocco, *was never once consulted as to the best approach which might dispose Noguès favorably toward the landings of November 7, 1942.* There was not only no consultation thereon but the legation was never afforded the opportunity to offer its comment on the means chosen in the light of its special familiarity with Moroccan problems.

Aware that the operation was imminent, I waited in vain for an invitation to express my views. With my deepening concern over the failure to ask for an expression of these, I at length drafted a telegram some ten days before November 7 suggesting that a military officer of high rank be assigned to the legation charged with conveying to Noguès some hours in advance a personal message from me assuring him of the serious character of the operation in view. I then committed the gravest error of my professional career in permitting the military attaché to dissuade me from dispatching it on the grounds that it could have no useful purpose inasmuch as every detail incident to the landings had already been determined.

Instead of the delegation of an officer of a rank commensurate with the importance of the message to be communicated, a junior vice consul from Casablanca was sent to acquaint General Noguès on the night of November 7 with Operation Torch. He was deputed for this task not only with no prior intimation to the legation but without even the prior knowledge of his own immediate chief, Consul General Russell! Here is the balance sheet of that truly Alice-in-Wonderland error: AMERICAN CASUALTIES—killed, 531; wounded, 1,054; missing, 237; FRENCH CASUALTIES—killed, 651;

wounded, 553. I do not affirm that had the legation been consulted the result would have been different, but it seems reasonable to conclude that it could not possibly have been worse.

With the strict hierarchical conceptions of a high-ranking French officer, Noguès was inevitably bound to judge the importance of the message conveyed to him by the rank of the messenger. As the Sultan's Minister for Foreign Affairs, the only authorized channel of communication with him from the American Government was the American Legation in Tangier. When it was announced to him that a junior vice consul, attached not to the legation but to the consulate general at Casablanca, had appeared at the residency bearing letters to the Resident General and the Sultan from President Roosevelt, Noguès could only conclude that he was being made the victim of a farce. To the uninitiated in diplomatic protocol, it is important to emphasize, for the better understanding of Noguès' reaction, that the consulate general in Casablanca might properly communicate with the Resident General only through the legation in Tangier. In consequence, Noguès refused to receive an emissary who was not accredited by the legation and who had the lowest rank in the American foreign service and directed an aide to take delivery of the letters. Upon reading them, wholly unconvinced of the seriousness of their import, he concluded that it was all a bluff. After consulting with French naval authorities, who reported that no important forces had been sighted off the coast, he was persuaded that he had to deal with nothing more than a commando raid. Preoccupied with his responsibility to preserve Morocco from German hands, he gave orders to resist, as he had so repeatedly warned me he would. Noguès had taken the most tragic decision of his long and honorable career.[7]

In *Roosevelt and Hopkins* Robert Sherwood has written: "Roosevelt attached great importance to Eisenhower's confession of astonishment at the situation as he found it in North Africa; it did not even remotely resemble prior calculations."[8] Sherwood adds that this admission indicated there must have been something wrong with his intelligence service. He remarks further that notwithstanding the fact that "the headquarters of Robert Murphy in Algiers and all the American consulates in that area and in Spanish Morocco were centers of Intelligence with large staffs," Eisenhower was amazed when the local French failed to hail Giraud as a conquering hero and that "this led to a display of political crudity which made the United States Government look ridiculously amateurish."

Now these are very fine words but they do not correspond with all the facts—except in one particular: our display of political crudity, about which there can be no disagreement. Sherwood has mistakenly confused the legation in Tangier, a post of political observation for the whole of Morocco, with a consulate in Spanish Morocco, but this is a detail of small importance, except as it reveals a certain unfamiliarity on the part of Sherwood with the Moroccan background. Of far more moment is Sherwood's failure to take into any account that President Roosevelt and General Eisenhower had abundant warning from the legation of the attitude of the French authorities and, in particular, of General Noguès.[9]

If this lack of coordination had tragic results in the circumstances attending the landings themselves, it was no less apparent in the events immediately following. Close on the heels of the landings a veritable witches' cauldron was brewed in Algiers. Admiral Jean Darlan, on a visit there to a son who was ill, was invited to take his seat, after the manner of Banquo's ghost, at the deliberations, presided over initially by General Mark Clark and subsequently by General Eisenhower. At this time Darlan was recognized, instead of Giraud, as the supreme French authority in North Africa.

On November 11, while these events were taking place and fighting was still in progress in Morocco, I received a telephone call from the residency in Rabat conveying to me General Noguès' desire for my urgent presence. A little later there was another call, informing me of a suspension of arms and repeating Noguès' request. Still a third message asked that I postpone my visit until November 13 as Noguès had been unexpectedly called to Algiers.

General Noguès was his old accustomed self, as cordial and friendly as ever, when I called on him on the afternoon of the thirteenth. He observed that he had sent for me in view of our close association over a considerable period of time as soon as there had been a suspension of arms on the eleventh. This decision had been made possible by his receipt on the tenth from Marshal Pétain of full powers as the representative of legitimate French authority in North Africa. Following the suspension of arms, he had been summoned to Algiers for conferences with the American and French authorities there, from which he had returned only a few hours earlier. As I was

in complete ignorance of the important decisions that had been
taken there, he was good enough to outline these to me.

General Mark Clark had presided at the first meeting with the
participation of Sir Andrew Cunningham, Admiral Darlan, Robert
Murphy, and General Giraud. According to Noguès' account, he
had found Clark most difficult. As for Giraud, Noguès had refused
on this first meeting to take the hand of this "dissident" who had
violated his oath as an officer in opposing the Marshal. For the same
reason the omission of any invitation to de Gaulle to the conference
had been particularly well received. It had been reported that he
might be invited, but no French officer present would have welcomed one who had refused to accept the armistice agreed to by
Pétain, French chief of state.

In a second meeting presided over by General Eisenhower, who
had arrived from Gibraltar, the proposal had been approved by all
those present that he, Noguès, should remit to Darlan the full
powers delegated to him by Marshal Pétain on November 10 while
Darlan was in American custody and that Darlan should issue a
proclamation in the name of the Marshal assuming responsibility for
French interests in North Africa. Thus there would be no "dissi-
dence" inasmuch as the authority conferred on Darlan would have
passed in legitimate succession from Pétain to Noguès and thence to
Darlan.

While in Algiers he had telegraphed the Marshal on the night of
November 12–13 requesting his accord with Darlan's designation, as
well as with the suspension of arms which had been concluded
between the French and American authorities. A very short time
before my appearance he had received a reply to this telegram of
which he subsequently gave me a copy. It bore the heading "Telegram of the Marshal of November 13, 14 hours" and this text:
"Reference telegram 50803 of November 12, 1942 from General
Noguès. Secret accord Marshal and President [Laval] but before
replying officially the occupying authorities are being consulted." [10]

In the course of our conversation I asked Noguès point-blank
why French forces had opposed us both in Morocco and Algeria
while failing to defend Tunisia against the Germans. His reply was
that such action was in compliance with "orders of the Marshal." He
thought his resistance had been indirectly of some advantage to us.
Vichy had telegraphed him on Sunday morning, November 8, that
the Germans wished to send troops by air to Morocco to assist in its

defense. He had replied that he could not answer for the loyalty of the French forces under his command in such an event. Our Western Task Force had been greatly favored in Morocco by an unusual absence of surf and an extremely quiet sea, as well as by a light fog which had obscured observation of our ships.

After my interview with Noguès I dined that evening with General George Patton in Casablanca. At his request I had obtained from Noguès an assurance that General Émile-Marie Béthouart, who had been imprisoned after an abortive coup at American instigation against Noguès the night of the landings, would be dealt with to the satisfaction of Generals Eisenhower and Patton. I had also arranged with the Resident General for Patton to be presented to the Sultan on either the sixteenth or the eighteenth, as he might desire.

Upon returning to Tangier on the sixteenth, I telegraphed Washington that it would be difficult to exaggerate the consternation into which most of the French in Morocco had been thrown by our recognition of Darlan. This was well summed up in a letter Clarac had addressed to Giraud in which it was stated: "French unity is threatened by exclusion of the Gaullists. Admiral Darlan, so long detested, and a symbol of Franco-German collaboration, hardly seems qualified morally to lead North Africa in a struggle on the side of the Anglo-Americans."

What considerations shaped an American policy which caused us to throw our support to Darlan immediately after the landings when the French were found to be opposed to the acceptance of Giraud owing to his lack of legitimate authority? Roosevelt defended the choice on the grounds of expediency, adding that the deal with Darlan had been made to save lives and gain time in the mopping up of Algeria and Morocco. Eisenhower, in *Crusade in Europe*, has presented a most persuasive account of the reasons for choosing Darlan, of which one of the most controlling was the vexed problem of legitimacy. Churchill justified the decision in his memoirs and it was approved by Stalin.[11] These are weighty authorities. Yet, notwithstanding the official public pronouncements blessing Darlan, public opinion expressed itself, at least in the free world, almost unanimously against the nomination.[12]

Outside the jurisdiction of the American military and civil authorities in Algiers and of Patton in Morocco, I sent home telegrams on the situation as we in Tangier saw it. They differed sharply at times from Patton's view. After drawing the attention of Washington repeatedly to the compelling necessity of instituting some effective control over the ingress into and egress from Morocco of notorious collaborationists and enemy agents, I was instructed to confer with Patton and come to some mutual agreement with him on the subject. I did so and an end was quickly put to a situation which had been crying for remedy. Shortly afterward when I called on him he took me sharply to task for occasioning him to spend so much time answering inquiries from the War Department growing out of my reports. He had no answer when I asserted that I had the same right to report directly to the State Department as he to the War Department. I reminded him that I was at pains to furnish him with copies of everything I sent and that I was scrupulously careful to give the source of my information. At this he banged his fist in a violent blow on the table and fairly shouted: "The trouble is you are too damned careful."

I might also have reminded him that I was never given access to any of his political reports as he was to mine, but it would have been to wave a red flag at a raging bull.

On a later occasion Patton requested that I arrange a meeting for him with General Orgaz, who proposed that Patton lunch as his guest at Larache in the Spanish Zone.[13] Patton had originally expressed a desire that I be present, and Orgaz was insistent to that effect. Shortly before the scheduled encounter Patton telegraphed me that on reconsideration he preferred that I not attend. Consulting Washington, I pointed out that Patton had no jurisdiction in Spanish Morocco and that the maintenance of cordial relations with the Spanish High Commissioner was of more concern to the legation than was pleasing the American commander. The Department of State agreed. At the desire of Orgaz I met him on the day fixed at the frontier, and while he remained on the Spanish side I waited on the opposite frontier to accompany Patton for his presentation to Orgaz. When Patton caught sight of me, his face blanched with anger. He strode forward, deliberately ignoring my greeting as I fell into step alongside. I explained that I was present under specific instructions of the State Department as well as at the specific behest of Orgaz. The frown disappeared from his face as he grasped my hand warmly. Great soldier that he was, he understood orders. However, if looks could have killed, I would have been dead before I could have offered my explanation.[14]

The American naval authorities in Morocco had requested me to intervene with General Orgaz to prevent firing by Spanish Moroccan shore batteries on American planes and blimps in hot pursuit of Axis submarines taking refuge in Spanish Moroccan waters. I telegraphed Washington of my intention to raise the question with Orgaz in three days in the absence of instructions to the contrary, repeating my telegram as a courtesy to Algiers. The first I learned that Algiers opposed such a move was in a telegram from Washington, handed to me as I was leaving for Tetuán, expressing agreement with Algiers that it would more properly be the subject of a démarche by our ambassador in Madrid. I was so confident of the contrary that I ignored the instruction, proceeded to Tetuán, and readily obtained Orgaz' agreement. Ambassador Carlton J. H. Hayes in his *Wartime Mission in Spain, 1942–1945* later testified that Orgaz' decision was of material assistance in obtaining similar assurances from the Spanish Government in Madrid.[15]

Our deal with Darlan had left the French in a state of confusion as to our political aims. Followers of de Gaulle, instead of being welcomed in Allied ranks, were the subject of persecution, while the most reactionary elements, including notorious collaborationists who had openly cooperated with the Germans, were accorded preferment by the American military authorities. A Frenchman who had edited a newspaper in Tangier subsidized by the Germans fled to Algiers immediately after the landings to escape the punishment the French were prepared to mete out to him. Once in Algiers he wormed his way so successfully into American confidence that he assumed editorship of a newspaper and was charged with the diffusion of radio propaganda in behalf of Allied war aims. When I communicated to Algiers the dismay of the French in Morocco at hearing the voice of this erstwhile traitor employed as a French spokesman, I was put off with vague phrases about not raking over old coals which might affect the Allied war effort. I countered, without success, by emphasizing the profound distrust which was being engendered about our political motives and the deep suspicion, already widespread because we ignored de Gaulle, that our purpose was the buttressing up of the discredited regime of Pétain.

I was aware that the reports with which I was bombarding Washington on the subject were as unpleasant reading for the President and the Secretary of State as they were for our military authorities, but I persisted in my course. A month after the landings, on December 13, 1942, I telegraphed with renewed insistence that as long as the equivocal political situation persisted in Morocco, discouragement and doubt were bound to deepen among our friends, with great moral damage both to the United States and to the Allied cause. At the time I did not exclude the possibility that I might one morning awake to find myself transferred and replaced by a more malleable agent. This was the expectation of many in the Department who were following my reports, and I did finally receive a mild admonishment from Mr. Hull.

The Secretary of State, in expressing concern about my telegrams, enjoined me to bear in mind the President's statement of November 17 that Darlan's appointment was a temporary expedient occasioned by the exigencies of war. The primary concern of the government was not with political problems but the attainment of victory by the quickest possible means. Finally, I was instructed to endeavor to combat the spreading of distrust of the Darlan arrangement, which was attributed to Axis propaganda, and to urge the desirability of a united front in prosecuting the war.

That we might win the war and lose the peace did not appear to have entered into anyone's calculations. I replied that there was no disposition to question the desirability of realizing a united front. It was precisely for that reason that those French with whom I was in touch were so disturbed. I added I was not competent to comment on Darlan's role. It appeared, however, to the Free French that if those identified with Vichy were to be accepted as working partners we had the obligation to insist that they cease the persecution of our friends of the Resistance and the lending of even indirect aid to our enemies.

The assassination of Darlan which followed could have offered no more persuasive testimony to the depth of feeling our policy had helped to develop. The way was now open for the succession of Giraud, an outstanding soldier whose political ineptitude proved most disappointing to his supporters. In the measure that we espoused Giraud politically, while keeping de Gaulle at arms' length, we bestowed upon the former the kiss of death. No nation, particularly one so proud as the French, could have been brought to welcome, even in its greatest extremity, a political leader imposed upon it by a foreign power, the more particularly when this involved the shunting aside of one around whom so many had rallied since 1940 as the symbol of an undefeated France. Our efforts to promote Giraud as a political leader were bound inevitably to enhance the popularity and strength of the Free French leader. Each successive interposition on our part in Giraud's favor pushed higher the stock of de Gaulle.

Once again we are confronted by the question of what factors were responsible for a misjudgment which was to have such unfortunate repercussions on the relations between France and the United States once de Gaulle became master of the destinies of his country. Whatever the reasons may have been, there is no doubt that both Roosevelt and Hull entertained an almost pathological dislike of de Gaulle. Reports from the American Embassy in London were distinctly unfavorable to many of the French with whom de Gaulle had surrounded himself there. In Vichy the American Ambassador, Admiral Leahy, discounted, as was perhaps natural in that atmosphere, the strength of de Gaulle's influence in France. By the character of his position Admiral Leahy was unlikely to be able to appraise de Gaulle's strength with the French Resistance.

The hostility prevailing in American official circles to de Gaulle was brought home to me very sharply in the spring of 1944 while I was in Washington on consultation. My first mention of his name when I was received by Secretary Hull evoked a tirade against the Free French leader. The thesis of the Secretary was that de Gaulle could not be trusted, and he instanced the duplicity with which de Gaulle had acted in the Free French take-over of Saint Pierre and Miquelon. When I was bold enough to remark that our opposition to de Gaulle was being widely interpreted in Morocco as indicative of an intention to support the Vichy regime in power after France's liberation, Hull's face flushed in denouncing it as de Gaullist propaganda. I countered that, on the contrary, this interpretation of our policy was being disseminated by Vichy sympathizers.

In Washington I dined with Admiral Jacques Fénard, who was in despair because of his inability to gain access to the White House to deliver a message to the President from de Gaulle. The only officers I found in the Department of State with any realistic appreciation of the French situation were A. A. Berle and H. S. Villard. On the eve of my return to Tangier, Leo Pasvolsky, special assistant to Secretary Hull, invited me to discuss my views of the situation with him. In the course of our conversation he assured me that, according to the Department's information, de Gaulle would not have the support of 15 per cent of the French people when our armies landed in France a few weeks later. I rose from my seat. "Goodbye, Leo," I observed. "I have my plane to catch. I can only say in parting: God help our government if we are formulating our French policy on any such false calculations." Leo was so impressed with the vehemence of my outburst that he asked me to send him a memorandum expressing my views on my return to Tangier. I knew better than to draft one myself; mine would make small impression. Instead I sent in an analysis by an outstanding retired French Army officer in Tangier. By that time the Department must have been giving ear to many other similar reports, for it was not long afterward that recognition was finally accorded de Gaulle in successive grudging doses, finally terminating with United States recognition of de Gaulle as legitimate head of the French state.

In June 1945 I was named American delegate to the International Conference in Paris on Tangier. With representatives of France, Great Britain, and Soviet Russia we drafted a new statute that we expected to endure at least a generation. It reflects the insecurity of our times that it was to last but little more than a decade owing to the subsequent independence accorded the Sultan of Morocco by France.

One of the first persons I met in Paris that summer was Henri de Malval, my Bucharest friend of twenty years earlier. He had just been released from Fresnes Prison, where he had been incarcerated by the Germans for his work with the Resistance.

With the collapse of France in 1940 Henri was serving as assistant French naval attaché in London. I was outraged when I had a letter from him stating that he had decided to seek a safe haven in a sumptuous villa placed at his disposal in Cannes by a friend in New York. My wife urged me to suspend judgment in the absence of a knowledge of all the circumstances, thereby proving that she was far wiser than I. My impatience with him boiled over again when he wrote and asked that I send him every week several food packages from Tangier. It was only at my wife's insistence that we must not abandon an old friend that I was moved to consent.

Malval, who was of a boastful disposition, could not avoid writing to his New York friend that as long as I was in charge of the legation in Tangier he had no material worries as he was being handsomely provisioned by me. We were not aware of it but all mail from Europe to the United States was being channeled through British censorship in Bermuda. His letter was intercepted, and the State Department was informed that one of their officers was violating the British blockade. It took a good deal of explanation on my part to persuade Washington that, owing to the special regime of Tangier, the packages I was sending for the subsistence of an old friend were acceptable even to the British post office there.

Perhaps the most piquant aspect of the affair was, as I learned from Malval in 1945, that the food packages which had occasioned the British complaint had been feeding British aviators escaping from France as well as British secret agents whom he had harbored at his Cannes villa. There he also had a secret radio station for communication with London. Malval's troubles began with the seizure by the Germans of a British agent who, with his wife, later attained great notoriety by their books about their wartime experiences. When found by the Germans, this agent was indiscreetly carrying a list of his Resistance contacts, and Malval's name was included. When the agent failed to appear at the rendezvous fixed, the worst was feared and Malval fled the villa and went into hiding, only eventually to be tracked down and captured in Paris. He had only escaped with his life owing to his knowledge of German psychology gained from youthful studies in Germany.

It was only after the war that I learned of a narrow escape that I may have had at the hands of the Germans. At a cocktail party in New York a guest was introduced to me who professed to know me well.

"I am sorry but I don't recall that we have ever met before."

"We haven't but I have good reason to know you."

"How is that?"

"In 1943 shortly after the landings you made a trip through Spanish Morocco from Tangier to Tetuán, Xauen, Melilla, and back by way of Oujda and Fez in French Morocco, did you not?"

"Yes, but how do you remember it so well?"

"I was in intelligence with the army, and we were intercepting and reading messages from the Germans in Spanish Morocco who were following your movements with keen attention. Fearful that they might be planning to bump you off, we debated whether to give you any warning. If we did and you abandoned your trip, the Germans might have suspected that we were breaking their codes. We decided in the end that you were expendable as your life was less important than our ability to read German secret communications."

I laughed half-heartedly. Then I asked more seriously: "Was this the application of a general policy of the army toward State Department officers?"

The hubbub was so great that I never caught his answer.

With the conclusion of the Tangier Conference in Paris I returned to Washington. Late in 1945 I was assigned to the Paris embassy to write *The American Foreign Service* (1948). When that was finished the following spring, I was offered an appointment as Minister to Saudi Arabia, where we then had only a legation, raised shortly afterward to an embassy. A pressing appeal was made for my acceptance. The capital, Jidda, was known to be lacking in the most ordinary amenities and subject to almost intolerable heat. I had been favored in Tangier, for almost five years, with one of the most interesting and desirable posts in the gift of the Department. It would have been bad grace on my part to have declined, even if service traditions had not stood in the way of such a refusal.

X

ARABIAN DAYS AND NIGHTS

AN AMERICAN AIR TRANSPORT plane deposited me on June 23, 1946, on a primitive airstrip at Jidda. Heat of an intensity unknown to me beat down in waves as if from an open furnace. There was no relief, no greenery or shade. A limitless expanse of sand and rock caught the sun's rays and reflected them with redoubled force. I was happy I had persuaded my wife not to venture out until the winter. There was no air conditioning. The Foreign Buildings Office, more interested in show places, had decided that it was not necessary. Not until we had been tortured with prickly heat did we finally succeed in obtaining air conditioning for the embassy, the chancery, and the staff's quarters. But we were to broil for two years before any relief was given us.

Before arriving in Jidda I had returned to Washington from Paris for instructions. There I had found Colonel Eddy, who, after service with me in Tangier, had spent two years as Minister in Saudi Arabia. We had a half hour together, with President Truman and Secretary of State Byrnes, in which we stressed the desirability of the pursuit by our government of a policy less aggressively pro-Zionist. With his receptiveness, Truman listened attentively and remarked to Byrnes: "I have never been a partisan of a Jewish State in Palestine."

Truman has offered testimony in his memoirs of the irresistible strength of Zionist demands. It was evident also in Republican circles. At a party given me by William Culbertson, whom I had known as American Minister to Rumania, I met Senator Owen Brewster. He had been making King Ibn Saud the subject of bitter attacks in the press. In my political naïveté I expressed to Culbertson the hope that Brewster could be persuaded to moderate his campaign to avoid prejudicing American interests in Saudi Arabia. Culbertson grunted. "Don't you know he is seeking nomination as Republican Vice President? He needs for that Zionist votes."

On my way through Cairo to Jidda I had spent an evening with an old friend, Abdul Rahman el Azzam, whom I had sought out in

1931 as one destined to play a role in Egypt. He was now secretary general of the Arab League. Azzam gave me a letter to his father-in-law, Khalid Bey Gargoni, one of Ibn Saud's principal advisers. It went far in paving the way for that close confidence later extended me by the King and his entourage. This was all-essential when dealing with an absolute monarch who ruled a country without a press and without consideration of public opinion.

The evening of my arrival in Jidda I stood on the balcony of the embassy fronting the Red Sea and recalled with a sinking heart that I had agreed to remain two years in this inferno. I asked myself if I would have the fortitude to endure the discomforts—not for two years but even for as many months. It is proof of man's infinite capacity for adjustment that I remained not only two but four years.

Despite the discomforts and the absence of any normal distractions I became so fascinated by my work and the challenge it presented that an inner happiness was found more than compensating me for the material comforts wanting. There were no theaters, no hotels worthy of the name, and neither day nor night clubs. There were only some fifty foreign residents with whom to foregather. The sole distractions were weekly movies organized for the foreign community on the terrace of the embassy, swimming in the shark-infested waters of the Red Sea with a temperature comparable to that of tepid soup, and trolling in the embassy motor launch for fish. Happily, I had my library of several thousand volumes.

While in Paris in 1945–46 I had begun to form a collection of original editions of Restif de la Bretonne which was eventually to become one of the most complete existing. To occupy my leisure moments I undertook an annotated bibliography in French of Restif, published in 1949. It was the one intellectual pursuit available and in this I forgot all else.

Life otherwise was of primitive simplicity. In the four years in Saudi Arabia I never wore a coat or a tie. Formal dress was the Red Sea kit, comprising an open-neck white shirt, black cumberbund, and black trousers. At the traditional New Year's Eve party at Gelatly Hankey, a British trading organization, we often perspired at midnight even when so attired. Showers had no hot water spigot; the so-called cold one was always lukewarm. To escape dehydration we consumed a dozen salt tablets daily.

The Koran embodied the supreme law of the land, administered by the Wahabi sect of Islam. As Moslem fundamentalists, the Wahabis were of a conservatism and rigidity comparable to Southern Hard-Shell Baptists. When religious leaders objected to the introduction of the telephone, King Ibn Saud overcame their scruples by having the Koran read over a trial hookup to prove that it was not the work of the devil. When I offered to have Jidda sprayed from the air by an American airplane to rid the city of the intolerable swarms of mosquitoes and flies drawn by the filth, the authorities expressed hesitancy until the religious leaders were consulted. It was feared there might be objections on their part to interference with the inscrutable ways of Allah as manifested through the lowly fly.

I once sought approval for the organization of a swimming club and the erection of a steel net as protection against sharks and barracudas. Ten months after the question was raised the King's approval was given on condition the club would be open to Saudi Arabians and foreigners alike and men and women would be segregated. My answer was that Americans had been engaged in mixed bathing for some time in the waters around Jidda and that I would prefer to brave the sharks than the anger of my female compatriots if they were segregated. I reminded Sheikh Yussef, the Saudi intermediary, that men might dominate in Arabia but the situation was quite the reverse in my country. That was the last we heard of it.

Women were so far excluded from all Moslem social functions that the American, college-bred wife of a Saudi diplomat could not accept invitations to the embassy if men were present. It was taboo for a foreigner to inquire of a Saudi Arabian regarding the health of his wife. There might be inquiry about his sons but not about his daughters or his wife or wives. The Minister of Finance had four, established in a like number of identical adjoining homes where he passed his nights in strict rotation. It was against Koranic precepts that any preference be shown one wife over another. It was an exceptional mark of the intimacy I was eventually to develop with the King that he confided to me his practice of never keeping a wife beyond the age of thirty. The twenties was for him the most desirable age for a wife. He considered Christians singularly afflicted in being limited to one wife. When I remarked once that some found a way out by taking a mistress, he objected that in doing so they transgressed their holy book while the Koran, in permitting four wives and an indefinite number of concubines, was far more responsive to human nature and precluded the sexual immorality prevalent in the Christian world.

When my relations with him had become unusually close, he went so far, on one of my visits to his capital, to propose through one of his ministers that I accept a slave girl in my quarters during my stay. So signal a compliment was almost unprecedented, since the Moslem generally regards with abhorrence physical possession of a Moslem woman by an infidel. When I recounted the story to my French colleague and assured him that I had refused the offer, his comment was, "Only an American would."

The first official call I paid upon my arrival in Saudi Arabia was on the Acting Minister for Foreign Affairs, Sheikh Yussef Yassin. With a dearth of competent Saudi Arabians, most of the higher officials in the government were Syrians and Lebanese. Sheikh Yussef was no exception; he was a Syrian. Preoccupied as I was with making the best possible first impression, I wondered how I might apply my Near Eastern experiences and, in particular, my knowledge of the impatience of the Arab with that formal protocol which tends so often to imprison diplomatic practice. In the initial exchange of platitudes through my highly competent interpreter, Mohammed Effendi, I sized up my interlocutor as an exceedingly shrewd Levantine with the passion of that people for intrigue and the matching of one mind against another. While making these rapid calculations, I decided that, with Sheikh Yussef's obvious sense of humor, he would be taken with a bold and unconventional approach.

The amenities having been observed, I remarked that I had been struck by the most contradictory opinions expressed to me about him by friends in whom I had confidence. I added, while observing the slight lifting of his eyebrows by my unexpected candor, that one friend had informed me that he was the most difficult person in the government with whom I would have to deal; another had assured me with equal conviction that no one could be more reasonable than he. Pausing an instant to allow him to digest my untraditional gambit, I smiled and continued. "It happens that there is only one person in the world who can prove to me indisputably which of my counselors is right and which is wrong."

Sheikh Yussef was too trained a diplomat and too much an Arab to betray his reaction. His beady eyes fairly bored into mine with the intensity of his gaze and absorption in what I might say next. It was only when he was fairly spellbound with expectancy that I leaned over closer to him and uttered the clinching line. "That person," I concluded, "is yourself."

His face relaxed and he shook with laughter.

Two years later we were in the midst of highly complicated treaty negotiations over the renewal of the Dhahran Air Base Agreement. We had reached an impasse on one particular provision, after discussions back and forth. Suddenly he laid aside his papers. "Tell me," he said, smiling, "do you consider me an unreasonable person?" "Why, of course not, Sheikh Yussef, why would you even suggest that as my opinion of you?" He had never forgotten the opening gun I had fired; it had served to put him on his mettle and had cemented a mutual confidence between us which never altered.

I have always been puzzled by a knack I have had in gaining the confidence of foreigners. When leaving Cairo for Iran in 1934, I asked the Iranian Minister in Egypt, a close friend, as to how I might best make my way in his country. He laughed. "Just be yourself," he replied. "There is a transparent candidness about you which inspires confidence and is all that you need."

At the invitation of the King I flew to the oasis of Riyadh, where the court had its seat, three hours east of Jidda by air. Riyadh was a Moslem holy city to which access was had only by express invitation of King Ibn Saud. It comprised his palace and those of his thirty-odd sons, spacious structures of two stories of traditional mud-brick construction, and a guest house for distinguished foreign visitors. This last was situated a little outside the town across a normally dry wadi, sufficiently distant from the center so that visiting infidels would not come too closely under the notice of the fanatical Moslem inhabitants. I never ventured out of the guest house during my early visits to Riyadh except for royal audiences. My purpose was to avoid detracting from the dignity of my mission, which might have been compromised by idle curiosity more appropriate to a tourist than a diplomat. It was only in response to the express invitation of the King that in 1949 I made my first visit to the town.

Protocol attending an audience with His Majesty was much less formal than that of a European court. The one rigorous prescription was the wearing of the Arab robe and headgear on such occasions. Immediately upon the arrival of a foreign visitor a tailor waited upon him to take his measurements and deliver the required costume

as a gift. When I later accompanied George McGee, Assistant
Secretary of State, to Riyadh, he was outraged when he saw me
donning such a costume in the plane preparatory to our landing. In
the face of his protests I remarked that as long as I was ambassador I
intended to respect the King's wishes the better to serve my country's interests. If Washington had other ideas, I was prepared to
offer my resignation. George continued to fume until the court
tailor called to take his measurements for a costume. When it was
delivered, I observed, with an amusement which I was at pains to
conceal, the admiring look with which he regarded himself in a
mirror. I knew better than to make any observation either then or
when it was donned for our audience. Two days later, on our
departure, he placed his arm around my shoulders, expressing regret
that he had been so obtuse. He had come to see my conformity in
better perspective, as a mark not only of deference to the King but
also to make less conspicuous my presence in a Moslem holy city.
"You were right and I was wrong," George added in keeping with
his generous character.

When granting audiences, the King was seated in a large high-
backed chair at the farther end of a spacious audience chamber.
Around it, extending from his chair, ran a cushioned, narrow, low
divan on which visitors were ranged according to their rank. Alongside the chair was a telephone as well as an electric bell by which he
might summon a servitor from an anteroom. The only other decorations or furnishings were rich Persian carpets which covered the full
extent of the floor.

The King was an imposing figure more than six feet in height. He
moved with some difficulty owing to an infirmity in his legs and his
marked bulk. His most conspicuous features were his piercing lumi-
nous eyes. When greeting and conversing with a visitor agreeable to
him, his face was suffused with a graciousness almost tender in its
nature. Apart from Woodrow Wilson, Emperor Haile Selassie, and
General George Marshall, no one else ever made on me a comparable impression of greatness and nobility of character. Pure son of the
desert, he was without any formal education. His natural endow-
ment of exceptional astuteness and judgment of men, along with an
indomitable will, had enabled him to weld together in half a century
the warring tribes of the Arabian desert into the kingdom which
bore his name.

Before the First World War the Ottoman Empire extended nominally over the whole of the Arabian Peninsula, including Kuwait, Nejd, Hail, Hejaz, Muscat, Trucial Oman, and Yemen. Effective power in the central and eastern areas had fluctuated between two families, the Rashids of Hail and the Sauds of Nejd. With the overrunning of Nejd by the Rashids, Ibn Saud had taken refuge with his father in Kuwait. In 1900 with only a handful of followers, young Ibn Saud, with the hardihood and rashness of youth, had crossed the desert from Kuwait to Riyadh and entered it under cover of night. The next morning as the Rashidi governor left for morning prayers at a nearby mosque, he was taken prisoner and Ibn Saud gained mastery of the oasis. His first title was Governor of Nejd and Imam of the Wahabis. On the fall of the Ottoman Empire he assumed that of Sultan.

The principal rival in the way of Ibn Saud's control of the entire Arabian Peninsula was Hussein, Sherif of Mecca, of the Hashemite family. To T. E. Lawrence, Hussein appeared a more promising leader during the First World War than Ibn Saud. Under Lawrence's inspiration and with British support, Hussein proclaimed himself King of the Hejaz and Caliph. Incensed more particularly by this last, Ibn Saud overran the Hejaz and forced Hussein into exile. All that the British could salvage of Lawrence's Arab dreams was the installation of Hussein's sons, Abdullah as King of Jordan and Feisal as King of Iraq. Until subsequent events brought about easement of the feud between the Hashemites and the Sauds, Ibn Saud's preoccupation was to protect himself against Jordan and Iraq through close relations with the non-Hashemite Arab states of Egypt, Syria, and Lebanon.

During my time in Arabia no visitor of mark to Riyadh was permitted to leave short of three days. The first was occupied with a ceremonial courtesy call, the second was reserved for the transaction of business, and the third for formal leavetaking. For the Arab as for other Eastern peoples time is of no importance. What is of moment is the strict observance of customs in social relations which have been sanctified by traditional usage. No greater discourtesy might be shown a visitor than failure to offer him, immediately upon arrival, unsweetened Arabian coffee, served from brass beakers in small handleless china cups. It would continue to be poured until a wiggling of the cup indicated that no more was desired. In contrast with European courts, the visitor took the initiative in withdrawing from the King's presence after requesting permission.

Dining with the King on the terrace of his palace at Riyadh was always a colorful occasion. Included among the thirty or forty guests were usually exiles from other Arab countries who had found favor with the King for political reasons. Of these the most notable was Rashid Aly, who had been obliged to flee from Baghdad after collapse of the German *putsch* there during the war. The first time I met him was at the King's table. With a twinkle in his eye and as if to twit me in that teasing way in which he delighted, Ibn Saud pointed at one of the guests seated some distance away and remarked to me: "You know who that is? That is the famous Rashid Aly," and he chuckled in amusement that I and a former instrument of the Nazis should be seated at the same table. It no more incommoded me than did the distinguished British orientalist present on that and many other occasions, H. St. John Philby, to whom the King had long been attached. Philby had embraced the Moslem religion. Without abandoning his British wife who resided abroad, he had taken an Arab one as well, with whom he lived during his periodic sojourns in Riyadh. As between Lawrence and Philby, who had both played important roles in the Arab world during and immediately following the First World War, Lawrence had profited by his showmanship to project his image before the public and gain the part of prima donna. Philby, of more solid substance and greater modesty, had occupied a less conspicuous position but had had a more enduring influence. For all the fanfare accorded Lawrence in the West, his name had vanished from memory in Arabia, much as a flash flood which sweeps in spring through the desert and disappears in the sands.[1]

In probably no land of the Near East was the etiquette of dining more strictly defined, or managed with more dispatch, than in Arabia. Immediately after the arrival of guests coffee was served, and within a quarter of an hour thereafter they were invited to table. During my first years in Saudi Arabia we sat on the floor around the dishes, spread out on the carpet. The invariable diet of the country was mutton, chicken, rice, coarse but tasty bread, a few tasteless vegetables such as potatoes, onions, and beans, and, for dessert, fruit or cream caramel. Fingers generally served in place of cutlery. There were no alcoholic beverages, nor were women ever present. It was perhaps due to their absence that there was little exchange of conversation. The main preoccupation was that of eating and of getting it over with quickly. As each guest finished, except at palace dinners, he rose and made use of a beaker of water, a bowl, and a towel offered by servants for the cleansing of the hands. When all had made their way to the original place of assembly, coffee was again served. A few moments later a small brazier was passed, the fumes of which were wafted into the wispy beard which most Arabs bore or, in the case of beardless Christians, into the face. The serving of tea shortly thereafter was a signal for the guests to take their leave. From the time of arrival to that of departure it was rare that more than an hour elapsed. On the conclusion of the King's dinners perfume was sometimes offered for rubbing between the palms of the hands. On one such occasion, after my relations with His Majesty had assumed a friendly and almost familiar character, he remarked to me, with his addiction to teasing: "I should not have afflicted you with this perfume. I had forgotten you have no beautiful houri to embrace you tonight as I."

After Crown Prince Saud paid his first visit to the United States in 1947, he persuaded his father to introduce greater formality in the entertainment of visitors, seating them in chairs at table and providing knives and forks. It afforded the King great amusement. He informed me that he was prepared to adapt himself to the newfangled reforms of his son so far as seating himself in a chair but he would never give up eating with his fingers.

On my first visit to Riyadh I had been accompanied by Major General Benjamin F. Giles, retired, who was seeking permission to organize a domestic airline with American planes and personnel. We broached the subject together and obtained the King's permission to launch an undertaking which is still successfully operating for all the difficulties of its execution in a feudal state. As long as King Ibn Saud lived, not a plane was permitted to take off even on scheduled operation without his express approval. It was not unusual for a commercial flight to be diverted to accommodate some member of the royal family or a minister.

On the final day of a visit to Riyadh there was a ceremonial bestowal of gifts by one of the King's senior officials. On the occasion of my first audience with the King I was the recipient of a sword with a gold scabbard, which was offered to all newly appointed diplomatic chiefs of mission. Thereafter I never called on the King at Riyadh that I was not given a carpet, a watch, or a gold dagger and invariably a new Arab costume. In the end I was impelled to inform him that I would be obliged to suspend my visits unless he consented to abandon the practice of presenting me with a gift on each occasion. I had made him two gifts in return, but with his simple tastes it was not easy to find suitable ones within my means. My insistence recalled to him his experience with Philby, to whom he had once loaned two thousand gold sovereigns. When the King refused to accept their repayment, Philby faced him with an ultimatum: acceptance of the sovereigns or his withdrawal from the country. Ibn Saud laughed as he told me the story. "I liked him too much to lose him so I had to accept the sovereigns." It was his delicate manner of indicating that he was constrained against his will to conform with my desires.

It was an exceptional concession on the part of the King because the exchange of gifts is for the Arab a sacred rite. So traditional was it that upon my appointment the American Government made available a costly motor car as a gift for the King. A formal acknowledgment was received but that was all; the Arab considers it the height of bad taste to give thanks for a present, however costly, not through any lack of appreciation but to avoid giving embarrassment to the donor. It is a reflection of that great delicacy of feeling which distinguishes the people.

That autumn when my wife joined me I had a telephone call at the chancery from Sheikh Yussef to inform me that the King was on a visit to Jidda and would receive her within an hour. It was a singular privilege as hardly a half dozen Christian women had ever had an audience with him. I drove hurriedly to the embassy and, entering, shouted to my wife that she had a bare half hour to dress before being received by the King. For answer I heard a hysterical outburst of sobbing. Becoming calmer, she explained that it was the ordeal of dressing in intolerable heat rather than fright at the prospect which dismayed her.

Some days later we were at the airport when the Minister of Finance, a special confidant of the King who knew we would be there, approached me to confide that he had a small gift His Majesty intended for my wife. I suggested we go over to where she was standing. Upon unrolling a greasy newspaper he disclosed a jewel case containing a magnificent string of pearls. To have refused the gift would have been an insult. I reported the circumstances to Washington and asked for instructions. The State Department must have been as puzzled as I for I never had an answer. On this occasion there were no tears on my wife's part, either when receiving the gift or afterward during the Department's silence.

Following my first visit to the King, I continued on for two hours by air eastward to Dhahran, site alike of our air base and of the Arabian American Oil Company (Aramco) headquarters, in order to familiarize myself with their operations. My work was chiefly centered around them—when it was not plagued by the question of Palestine. The air base, the sole one left to us in the Near East at the end of the war, had only just been completed under an agreement concluded in 1945. That arrangement provided that the base would become the property of the Saudi Arabian Government on March 15, 1948, and contained an obligation on our part to provide training to Saudi Arabians to permit its eventual operation by them.

To my consternation I found that not a single step had been taken to that end. Even more disturbing was the news given me by the commanding officer at Dhahran that, following economy measures of the Pentagon, the Air Force complement had been reduced to a bare handful of officers and men. I had no knowledge of air or defense strategy but one glance at a map was sufficient to persuade me of the prime importance of Dhahran, situated on a land mass resembling a gigantic aircraft carrier, astride the Middle East, and close to one of the world's richest oil fields, in which we had a controlling interest. Upon returning to Jidda, I sent a series of telegrams to Washington emphasizing Dhahran's importance, the need of expansion rather than reduction, and the imperative necessity we were under to fulfill our contractual obligation to train Saudi Arabians if we desired to retain the base.

These efforts found no response in Washington until after the lapse of many months. At length, in 1947 a training program was instituted, and a very able officer, Colonel Richard J. O'Keefe, was sent to supervise it and to reorganize the base. Although we were established at opposite sides of the Arabian Peninsula, so quickly did he grasp the delicate political problems which were constantly arising and so eye to eye did we see that it was of great comfort to me to know that no difficulties would arise out of the air base operation to complicate our task as long as O'Keefe was in command. In view of his outstanding ability he was shortly made a brigadier general.

The chief source of problems was Palestine. The general background of the controversy as I viewed it at close hand from Jerusalem in 1923–25 and again in the Department in 1937–40 has already been presented. At the end of the Second World War it came once more to the fore at a meeting on February 24, 1945, between President Roosevelt and King Ibn Saud at Great Bitter Lake in the Suez Canal. At this interview Roosevelt gave his personal assurance not only that he would never take action which might prove hostile to the Arabs but, more important, that the United States would not change its policy toward Palestine without full and prior consultation with both Arabs and Jews. Nothing could have been more specific than these undertakings, which were renewed in writing in a letter of April 5, 1945, from President Truman to the King.

Let us examine how these obligations were observed in order to gain some understanding of the bitterness of the Arabs.

The Second World War had imposed a barrier to Jewish immigration into Palestine. With its termination the Zionists renewed their pressure for open access to that country. On the eve of the congressional elections in 1946 President Truman issued a statement favoring the immediate admission to Palestine of 100,000 Jewish refugees. Not to be outdone the Republican candidate, Dewey, asked why the number should be limited to 100,000. The British Government, dependent upon American aid, had no alternative but to acquiesce. Pandora's box had been opened. American Zionists were quick to take advantage of their unabashed wooing by both parties. One of their leaders, Rabbi Wise, went so far as to take Secretary of State Byrnes sharply to task in a letter of October 23, 1946, which found its way into print. "The State Department is not giving full support to the policy which the President's statement would seem to reflect," the letter charged.

It was in the midst of this new pressure campaign that the King sent for me only a few months after my arrival in Saudi Arabia. I flew to Riyadh in the plane the Air Force had placed at my permanent disposition. One of the engines failed on the take-off. But for the superb pilot, Jack Womack, we would both have lost our lives. This was not the only occasion on which my life was saved by him. Once he brought the plane down in a severe dust storm on an indistinguishable airstrip of sand, in a landing forced on us by lack of fuel and the gathering dusk.

On our way to Riyadh another time I happened to go into the cockpit to observe the navigation. After a while Jack indicated a chimney rock on an escarpment, the one landmark in that endless sea of sand. "We will bear to one o'clock now and will be in Riyadh in half an hour." My guiding spirit must have been with me that day. A year later I was accompanying Admiral Richard Conolly and a group of naval officers from Dhahran to Riyadh on a visit to the King. The pilot, who had made the flight but once, lost his way, so hopelessly that he began to circle in the endeavor to spot Riyadh. Fuel was running low. On an off chance that I might help, I entered the cockpit to have a look around. Ten minutes later I spotted the chimney rock. "Turn around," I said. "You are heading for Jidda. You will find Riyadh by bearing at one o'clock off the rock." We did, to the relief and amazement of the naval officers, who found it amusing—after we had touched ground—that a diplomat knew enough about navigation to bring admirals into port.

On the occasion of my visit to the King late in 1946 in answer to his summons I found him deeply concerned over the apparent yielding of American politicians to the Zionists in the United States. The King recalled the solemn assurance given him by President Roosevelt and expressed his apprehension that we might be headed in the pursuit of a policy pregnant with disastrous consequences in the Near East.

I was handed a letter for President Truman to which a response was forthcoming a few days later. The President's reply rejected the charge that the advocacy of the entry of 100,000 Jews into Palestine represented an action hostile to the Arab people or that there had been any failure on the part of the American Government to fulfill the assurance that no decision would be taken on Palestine without prior consultation with both Arabs and Jews. It was added that "during the current year there have been any number of consultations with both Arabs and Jews." Actually there had been none with the Arabs on the crucial question of immigration. And this was what was of greatest concern to the King. When I delivered Mr. Truman's reply, the King remarked that the Arabs would not object to the establishment on the Mediterranean coast of Palestine of a Jewish enclave. What the Arabs feared above all was that once a Jewish state was created extending over most of Palestine there would be no holding back Jewish pressure for further *lebensraum*. The existing limits of Palestine were, in his opinion, quite insufficient for that Jewish in-gathering which was the announced Zionist objective.

In the face of the pressure brought to bear on it, the British Government sought to shift solution of the Palestine issue to the United Nations. After the United States had announced on October 11, 1947, its support of a plan for the partition of the country, the plan was approved on November 29 by the bare two-thirds majority of the General Assembly required. This decision, according to James Forrestal, then Secretary of Defense, was one "fraught with great danger for the future security of" the United States.[2]

In his *Diaries* Forrestal describes the Zionists' lobbying on this occasion. So great was it that reports were widespread that it had extended to the exercise of undue pressure by American officials on foreign delegations to the United Nations to influence their voting. The State Department was at length obliged to take cognizance of these. All American diplomatic missions to Arab states were instructed to inform the governments to which they were accredited that neither the State Department nor the White House had interfered in any way in the vote leading to the adoption of partition.

In Jidda I made the communication to Prince Feisal, Foreign Minister, the most distinguished of the King's sons. He regarded me quizzically as I delivered it orally. When I had finished, he replied without hesitating an instant, "The only comment I can make is that the President must be sadly uninformed concerning the activities of his staff." He was referring to those of David Niles, who dealt with Jewish affairs. A member of the White House secretariat later remarked to me that a Zionist, such as Niles, might well have telephoned, without the knowledge of the President, to delegations of the United Nations to whom such a call would inevitably have carried the full weight of influence of the White House.

The General Assembly's resolution had no binding force until implemented. The storm subsequently unleashed by it in the Arab world gave pause both to the United Nations and to the United States. Reports from American diplomatic missions in the Near East were unanimous in expressing to the State Department the view that our espousal of the cause of the Zionists in Palestine would have as inevitable consequences open warfare between Arabs and Jews together with the loss of the good will built up over the years for the United States in the Arab world.

The cumulative effect of these reports, together with rejection of the partition of Palestine by the Security Council, brought about another reconsideration of American policy. The announcement on

At a luncheon offered by Aramco to Ibn Saud on his visit to Dhahran in 1947.
On the King's right and left are Emir bin Jaluwi and Ambassador Childs

The chancery of the American Embassy at Jidda about 1948

March 19, 1948, that the United States had decided to support a temporary trusteeship for Palestine, was followed by a statement of Secretary of State Marshall referring to the "vital elements in our national security involved." For the first time these were publicly taken into account by the government. A telegram from the Department informed me that the United States Government would not be swayed in consideration of the Palestine problem either by external or internal pressure.

The Arab League was not so easily impressed as was I by the apparent adoption on our part of a more neutral position. Abdul Rahman el Azzam, the secretary general, appeared on the scene from Cairo to consult with the Saudi Arabian Government on the position the Arab League should adopt. I assured him, invoking our friendship of twenty years, that I was convinced we were at long last to be guided by strictly American interests rather than the exigencies of American domestic politics. Edwin A. Locke came as the personal representative of President Truman to convey like assurances to the King and to me. Azzam was skeptical but impressed by the weight I assured him they might be given. I went to Riyadh and repeated the assurances on my part to the King. There were almost tears in the eyes of his counselors with the hopes thus raised. "We do not ask for American support of the Arab cause," I was told, "but only for impartiality."

In the meanwhile a bitter struggle, of which I was not apprised until later, was taking place in Washington between American policy makers, on the one hand, concerned with safeguarding American security interests in the Near East and party strategists of the Democratic National Committee, on the other, under the formidable pressure of the Zionists, whose influence counted in consideration of the party's fortunes. As a result American policy took another sharp reversal and on March 30, 1948, called for a special session of the United Nation's General Assembly to consider again the future of Palestine. I learned of this new development in Riyadh on the heels of the message I had been authorized to convey to the King to allay his apprehension. But for the personal confidence I enjoyed, I would have been treated as having deliberately connived at an effort to pull wool over the King's eyes.

Events now began to march with seven-leagued boots. The British, under constant harassment in the execution of the mandate by the United States, announced their intention to let the running sore burst and to withdraw from the country on May 14, 1948. When that day came the state of Israel was proclaimed. Forrestal has described in his *Diaries* the unseemly haste with which American recognition followed on the same day.[3] A minority had imposed its will on the government of the United States.

It is open to question whether the American Zionists who made their will felt were altogether representative of American Jews. Many Jews, undivided in their allegiance to the United States and far less vocal than the Zionists, had great misgivings as to the turn of events, including the subsequent displacement of the more than a million Arabs forced to flee Palestine. They were aligned with many other Americans who regarded with distress and apprehension the war which ensued between Arabs and Israelis, the assassination of the United Nations' mediator, Count Bernadotte, at the hands of Jewish terrorists, and, finally, the uneasy truce negotiated by an able and distinguished American, Ralph Bunche, which remains as insecure as when it was concluded.[4]

Some of these facts will be unfamiliar to the American public. Owing to a rigorous campaign of suppression little was published in the American press concerning the Arabs displaced in such large numbers following creation of the state of Israel. This hush-hush policy on the part of the press extended even to the administration, which was at pains to avoid publicity revealing any especially close relations with Arab states. In 1949 I made a tour of Air Force bases in the United States as the guest of the Air Force to inspect the training program for Saudi Arabian students posted at certain airfields in accordance with our commitments under the Dhahran Air Base Agreement. At Wichita Falls a newspaper sought an interview with me to ascertain the occasion of my visit. A public relations officer cautioned me that no information had been given to the press previously regarding the presence of Saudi Arabian students on the base and that before this could be made known special authorization would have to be obtained from Washington. In answer to a telephone call clearance was finally obtained for divulgence of the facts.

Some time later I was invited to speak at Randolph-Macon College on Arab-Israeli relations. As there are relatively few Zionists in Virginia, the newspapers in the state were not inhibited in reporting my talk at some length. Several wrote to me to express their satisfaction in being made acquainted with a background on which metropolitan news media had for long preserved a rigorous silence. What

I found particularly revelatory of a thirst for facts was an invitation from the American Council for Judaism in Richmond to repeat my talk before its Jewish members, disturbed at how the subject had been veiled in the past.

A single example will suffice to show how the nettlesome question of Palestine complicated my task. In the spring of 1949, on the heels of the creation of the state of Israel, it fell to me to negotiate a new Dhahran Air Base Agreement to replace the one which had expired. In that task I had the able assistance and counsel of General O'Keefe. Such was the bitterness which had been aroused by the support the United States had given to the creation of Israel that the first draft we proposed, at the instance of Washington, was rejected out of hand. As a means of mitigating Saudi Arabian insistence that the base be wholly under their control I hit upon a formula which I thought would respond to Saudi Arabian exigencies and would at the same time be acceptable to us. This was to confer upon O'Keefe a double function: one was that given him by the United States as commanding officer of United States forces at the base and the other, that of exercising control of civil aviation at the base as agent of the King.

In the light of the bitterness engendered against the Jews the Saudi Arabian authorities insisted that the new agreement stipulate that no American personnel should be posted to Dhahran unacceptable to the Saudi Arabian Government. This amounted in effect to the exclusion of Jews from our personnel in the Air Force at the base. A great deal was subsequently made of this by American Zionists, who ignored the sovereign right of a government to prescribe measures governing the entry of persons into its territory. It was either the acceptance of such a condition or the abandonment of the base. Aramco was also obliged to conform with the wishes of the local government in this regard or else to relinquish its concession.

All this reflected the profound antagonism against the Jews aroused in the Arab world by events in Palestine. The Christian head of an American enterprise in Jidda was given twenty-four hours to leave the country for having recommended to his head office the establishment of trade between the New York office and Israel. Two American Jews traveling on official business for the State Department were denied entrance to the country. There was no basis in international law for any protest.

So deep was the fanaticism prevailing that it was not alone Jews who suffered disabilities. The performance of marriage rites between Christians was not allowed nor was the public holding of Christian religious services. Through a tacit understanding these had been permitted under the auspices of Aramco and the Air Force in a private hall but without the display of any religious images. An officer of the embassy who was so rash as to raise the issue officially with the government during my absence drew in reply a formal note banning even private services. It was only as the result of a pressing appeal on my part to the King that the note was withdrawn. I argued that if sent to Washington it would prove in the highest degree embarrassing in provoking official cognizance of an issue that we had best resolve informally as we had in the past. As a result private services were resumed.

We were confronted by conditions and not theories, and we had to accommodate ourselves to them, not in the spirit of crusaders but of realists. We sought in doing so to exercise a spirit of understanding. O'Keefe informed me once that his principal medical officer had confided to him that he was Jewish on his mother's side and had been sent to Saudi Arabia by the Air Force in ignorance of the fact. As O'Keefe assured me that he was a most able officer and one on whose discretion he could rely, as well as one who had many friends among the Arabs, it was agreed to take no steps for his recall. He subsequently accompanied me on a mission to Yemen and was received both by the Imam and by King Ibn Saud.

If Palestine injected poison in our Arab relations, it happily did not affect the operations of Aramco. This was due not alone to the importance it had assumed in the country's economy but also to the enlightened policies of that company. The great oil development in the Persian Gulf area dated from the beginning of the century with the D'Arcy concession in Iran. After the First World War the Iraq Petroleum Company was formed with American, British, and French capital for the exploitation of oil in Iraq and Trucial Oman. In Kuwait the concession was a joint enterprise of the Anglo-Persian and Gulf Oil companies. Other American capital was drawn to the scene, and there ensued exploitation of oil at Bahrein by Standard of California and the Texas Company (Caltex). On May 29, 1933, the former obtained exploration rights in Saudi Arabia, with the later participation of the Texas Company, Standard of New Jersey, and Socony-Vacuum. The first oil was discovered in 1938, and by 1946 daily production had risen to 150,000 barrels. Four years later it was half a million barrels daily, and by 1969 daily production had grown to three million barrels. According to oil experts, such production may continue for another century.

After the Second World War there was a scramble for concessions in the Neutral Zone between Kuwait and Saudi Arabia which is under the joint ownership of those two countries. I was astonished to be informed one day by Sheikh Yussef at the Foreign Office that owing to my personal interest and that of my government in the application of the Superior Oil Company the King had decided to award it the concession in that area. I was aghast at the news, the more so as I had been at scrupulous pains, I thought, to avoid indicating any preference between the Superior Oil Company and the Getty company, which were competing for the Neutral Zone concession. When the Superior representative planned an initial visit to Jidda, he had written and requested, in the absence of a suitable hotel, that I put him up at the embassy as the British had done in the case of a British representative of Superior. When I replied expressing my regret, the company complained to the Department about my lack of cooperation. The Department informed the company that my action was approved as it would have been inappropriate for me to have acceded to the request. When I informed Sheikh Yussef of this background, he readily agreed to acquaint the King with our conversation. As a result, some months later the Saudi Arabian Government accepted the Getty offer for this immensely valuable concession. It is doubtful if that company ever knew of the circumstances here recounted.

The incident illustrates the great part personal influence plays in Arab decisions. It points up also the great prudence that a diplomat must exercise.

Prudence was incumbent not only on diplomats but also on American commercial interests dealing with Saudi Arabia. It was in the exercise of prudence, tact, and farsightedness that the most important private American interest in the country, the Arabian American Oil Company had gained so solid a position. It had done so by avoiding the errors committed by oil companies in Mexico and by the Anglo-Iranian Oil Company in Persia. Instead of abusing the power acquired, Aramco had been a model of restraint. Hospitals, schools, and on-the-job training had been introduced at an early stage. In these and in other activities, such as the housing of its workers and the facilities offered them, the company had sought to anticipate rather than to follow government desires.

In consequence, Aramco gave me few cares. The one exception occurred in 1949–50 when the Saudi Arabian Government made known its desire for a fifty-fifty share in profits after the example of Venezuela. It came coincident with a like demand on the Anglo-Persian Oil Company by Iran. In view of the importance of the issue to the American Government, Assistant Secretary George McGee convoked a conference on the subject early in 1950 at the State Department. As spokesmen for Aramco, R. G. Follis, chairman of the board of Standard Oil of California, and Brewster B. Jennings, president of the Socony Vacuum Oil Company, attended. The Department's spokesman was McGee, assisted by Richard Funkhouser, petroleum adviser of the Department, and me.

Follis entered the conference in a hostile and defiant mood. In the face of the masterly presentation of the problem by McGee, Follis took the floor in the end to announce that all his objections were overcome and that he would recommend acceptance of the fifty-fifty formula. As we emerged from the conference, Funkhouser remarked that he would send a telegram at once to the embassy in London to apprise the British. "Persian pressure will now become irresistible. Let us hope the Anglo-Persian Company will display the statesmanship shown this morning by Aramco." Unfortunately it was not to be. The result was the cancellation of that concession by the Iranian Government shortly thereafter.

As my four years in Saudi Arabia neared their end, I became increasingly concerned with the disorder in the finances of the country. Although the income in 1946 from all sources, including pilgrimage and customs dues and oil royalties, did not exceed twenty million dollars, it was mounting almost astronomically from increased oil production. Yet these expanding resources continued to be squandered with a prodigality which for the first time was exciting murmurs on the part of the population. Millions were being disbursed in palaces for the King's sons and favorites with an appearance of reckless abandon, made possible by the absence of modern accounting procedures, with consequent widespread corruption. In Saudi Arabia, as in many Near Eastern countries, civil servants were paid only nominal salaries, but with these went a recognized prescriptive right to supplement them from the public till. By 1949 the situation had reached such proportions as, in my view and that of others, to threaten the stability of the Saudi dynasty. Our stake in the country was too great for us to stand idly by and allow developments to run their course toward disaster.

The King had given me an opening on one occasion when I lunched with him in Jidda. I remarked how impressed I had been that, instead of erecting nonutilitarian monuments to glorify his reign, he was devoting some of his revenues to public works, such as a railway from Damman to Riyadh, port developments at Jidda and Damman, and municipal electric power and water supply systems. "A sovereign," he replied, "who does not place the interests of his people before his own is not worthy to rule."

I determined to act on my own without consultation with Washington, which might have been reluctant to approve a *démarche* on my part suggestive of interference in the domestic affairs of the country. After taking counsel with and receiving the hearty blessing of Fred Davies and Floyd Ohliger of Aramco, at Dhahran, and Garry Owen, the company's representative in Jidda, I sounded out Crown Prince Saud, who was in Dhahran at the time. He expressed warm approval of the initiative I proposed to take, whereupon I proceeded to Riyadh to see the King.

I recalled to him the conversation we had had on public works and announced that I intended to speak, not officially as ambassador, but as one of his own people or as the son he had come to consider me. As it was hopeless to discuss economic theory with the King, I remarked, the better to bring home my thesis, that Saudi Arabia had evolved overnight from a simple shop to a store with many ramifications, while still retaining the accounting methods of a bazaar merchant. For all my efforts I perceived that I was making no impression. Finally I resolved to throw in my last chip the more effectively to convince him of the crucial importance I attached to my observations.

"Your Majesty," I observed, "I ask only that you call in your sons and your principal ministers. If, after questioning them, you find I have misinterpreted the situation, you have only to inform my government that you no longer have confidence in me and ask for my replacement."

Fuad Bey Hamza, who had been interpreting and had amazed me by whispering words of encouragement as I proceeded, came to the translation of my last sentence. The King interposed his hand imperiously. "No, I will not have it suggested that such a situation will ever arise." He laid his hand on my arm: "I have always considered you a friend; today you have given me decisive proof."

For all his expression of confidence I was wholly unable to represent the situation in a manner that he might grasp. His argument was that he was a Bedouin who had been brought up in the simple ways of his people and that he was much too old to change them. When I reported the results to Washington, I was gratified that instead of being chided I was commended for the initiative I had taken. I would have been more pleased to have achieved some concrete results. That the seed thus planted did not fall altogether on barren ground was later evidenced by the eventual employment of an American financial adviser and the establishment of a central bank.

The evolution of Saudi Arabia from the feudal state in which it has for so long remained is a slow process but it is bound to become accelerated under the impact of the outer world which thunders over and about it after a sleep of centuries. Since my departure Prince Saud has succeeded his remarkable father as King. He, in turn, has been replaced by his brother, now King Feisal, certainly the most notable of his father's many sons. I have been away from Saudi Arabia too long to venture any predictions, but if we judge on the basis of what has occurred elsewhere, it must be plain that unless the Saudi Arabian people are given a greater share of their birthright accruing from the increasing oil royalties, an eruption is inevitable.[5] The British wisely persuaded the Sheikh of Bahrein to allocate a third of his oil royalties to public works, a third to a reserve fund to afford revenue when oil is exhausted, and a third for the expenditures of the Sheikh and the state. In the absence of similar measures in Saudi Arabia the storm will break there sooner or later, as it has in Iraq and Egypt.

In 1950 I completed four years in Saudi Arabia. When assigned there the Department had assured me it would be for only two years. At the end of my second year, in 1948, the situation involved so many delicate factors consequent upon our recognition of the state of Israel that I volunteered to remain for a third year. I did so again in 1949 to spare a new chief of mission from assuming the post in the exacerbated state of Arab-American relations. In 1950 I was pressed by Washington to remain for a fifth year. By that time, however, my vitality had been so sapped by temperatures rising at times as high as 136 degrees that I was compelled to decline, particularly as there were no longer compelling political reasons for the prolongation of my stay.

The King's reaction to the news that I was leaving was quite characteristic. When he received me a few days after it had been made known to the local government, he announced categorically that he had no intention of allowing me to leave. In a tone which implied that I was as much subject to his orders as to those of my government he added that he had sent a telegram to his ambassador in Washington to convey to the American Government his insistence that I stay.

I expressed deep gratification with these marks of his confidence but informed him that there was no possibility of obtaining any countermanding of my orders. It was brought home to me as I observed him that sovereigns have a psychology differing fundamentally from that of ordinary mortals. The perplexity on his face was almost pathetic; the idea that his orders would not be executed was one which he found it difficult to grasp. It was only after I hastened to add that the state of my health was what stood in the way of my remaining that his countenance relaxed. He placed his hand on my arm and stated that under the circumstances he would not stand in my way.

He was a very great monarch and a very great man.

XI

QUEEN OF SHEBA AND LION OF JUDAH

I N 1946 I had been appointed to serve as first American Minister to Yemen concurrently with my duties at Jidda. The ancient land of Yemen, Saba of the Bible, once the seat of the Queen of Sheba, lies in the southern part of the Arabian Peninsula. It was ruled in 1946 by Imam Yahya, some eighty years of age, the despotic successor in a dynastic line which had endured a thousand years. The isolation of the country was such that probably not a hundred Christians had ever set foot in it. The first diplomatic representation had been admitted only a few months before my own visit when my French colleague at Jidda had presented his letters of credence.

Yemen has been described as a country "rushing headlong into the Middle Ages." By comparison Saudi Arabia was a modern state. Those in a position to know have told me that the subsequent revolution in Yemen and declaration of a republic in a part of the country have not altered its feudal character.

To reach it was in itself an adventure. I flew to Kamaran Island, then administered by Britain, in the Red Sea, whence a British launch conducted me to the three-mile limit of its offshore waters. There native skiffs were awaiting me. On approaching the shore I had to be borne to land on the backs of porters owing to the shallowness of the waters. A waiting truck was our means of conveyance to a government resthouse in Hodeida for an overnight stay. From there a car of especially high clearance made the fantastic ascent to the highlands by way of a river bed, in the absence of a proper road, to the foothills, and thence along what passed for a road to the plateau. A journey of 120 miles took us two days.

Before reaching the capital San'a, at a height of some 5,000 feet, the government representative accompanying me had to telephone for permission from the Imam for us to enter. The sight of foreigners was so unusual that our progress attracted hundreds crowding the way. In the city itself I was never able to quit the comfortable guest house provided for our accommodation without being followed by crowds of the curious.

No city I know of has so distinctive an appearance as Yemen's capital. From afar the many stone buildings, rising to a height of from six to eight stories, present a modern skyline. On closer inspection the modernity disappears. Yet no place could be more attractive than San'a, with the rich vegetation surrounding it which springs from the heavy seasonal precipitation swept in from the Indian Ocean. The thick forests of the interior offer striking contrasts with the utter barrenness of Saudi Arabia.

Only a few hours in San'a sufficed to make me aware of the cat-and-mouse game Yemenis delight in playing with foreigners. I was first assured the Imam was ill and that it was doubtful if he would be able to receive my letters of credence. After a day or two of delay to exhaust my patience it was suggested in a note from the Foreign Minister that the diplomatic secretary of my mission, Harlan Clark, who as consul at Aden had made an earlier visit to San'a, should be deputed to meet with a Yemeni representative to transact any business we had to propose. I refused to fall into that trap. Once the Yemenis learned we had nothing concrete to offer, there would have been no inducement for the Imam to receive me, and I did not relish returning to Jidda and having to report failure in my mission to be received officially by the Imam. When I replied that the formula was unacceptable because I alone was authorized to deal with the government, the Imam's health took a suspicious turn for the better. Soon afterward I had word that I would be received by the sovereign at his palace on the following day.

At the audience, less impressive than those of King Ibn Saud, the Imam announced that owing to his age and infirmities he would depute his son, Prince Hussein, to serve as his spokesman with me.

Imam Yahya's fate was that of many Near Eastern monarchs. A year and a half later in a short-lived insurrection both he and Prince Hussein were assassinated, along with many of the notables I had met. Upon succeeding to the throne, Crown Prince Ahmed, who owed his life to his residence in Ta'izz in the south, refused to move to San'a. It availed him nothing: he was himself assassinated in 1962 after succeeding to the imamate.

During the best part of a week I conferred with Prince Hussein at his home. During this time I outlined what the United States had in

view in Yemen. His Highness was attentive but quite uncommunicative, offering no slightest comments. When I had finished my expo-
sition, the Prince informed me that he would give the Imam a full
account of my remarks and that answers to the various questions
raised would be forthcoming on the day preceding that fixed for my
departure.

When I called on that day at the appointed time in the morning,
the Foreign Minister received me and we waited for the Prince. An
hour elapsed and then a second with no sign of Prince Hussein. I
then took my leave, leaving the Foreign Minister in considerable
confusion. An hour later the Minister called at the guest house to
present Prince Hussein's excuses: he had been summoned by his
father to the palace. No explanation was forthcoming of his failure
to inform me of the fact sooner. I was assured that if I would be
good enough to return at three o'clock that afternoon he would be
awaiting me. As a measure of reparation, I was offered access to the
Royal Library of Arabic manuscripts, which no foreign visitor had
ever previously been permitted to view.

At three I returned to Prince Hussein's home, where I found the
Foreign Minister but not His Highness. When he had still not
appeared after fifteen minutes, I informed the Foreign Minister that
I had an appointment with the Lebanese delegation in San'a and
that I would never contemplate being so altogether lacking in
courtesy as to keep the head of that mission waiting for so much as a
minute. My appointment actually was two hours later. The Foreign
Minister was embarrassed and unable to offer other than vague
explanations of the Prince's absence. If I had been in Yemen longer,
I would have better appreciated that his conduct was entirely in
keeping with Yemeni character.

I strolled about the town until it was time for my call on the
Lebanese and, that concluded, I paid a visit to one of the two
European residents of the city, an Italian doctor. While we were
having tea, an excited messenger from the Prince, who had learned
my whereabouts, appeared to state that his master wished to pay me
a visit at the guest house, an unheard-of departure from Yemeni
protocol. I answered with studied indifference that it would be at
least another hour before I would be there. To emphasize my lack
of eagerness to receive the Prince, I lingered beyond the hour and
then, instead of returning in my car, made my way back on foot.
The servants at the guest house presumably had instructions to give

notification of my arrival for it was not long thereafter before the Prince made his appearance. He was not alone but was accompanied by the entire Yemeni cabinet. It was handsome acknowledgment of the lesson I had conveyed by indirection. Prince Hussein lingered so late in the evening that it was close to midnight before he took leave with his deputation.

To acquire a more thorough knowledge of the country I proposed to return to Jidda by proceeding overland south to Taʻizz, where Crown Prince Ahmed resided, and thence to Aden. There was a road only to the foothills of the central mountain range. A car conducted us there, where a convoy of pack mules had been provided to transport us across the mountains into a rich populous valley. After an overnight stop in a village at the foot of the mountains we had traversed, we continued to the eastern extremity of the valley at Ibb, where we were received at lunch by Prince Hassan, the local governor. The only radio in this entire region was in his possession. There was not a newspaper in the country, and the introduction of those published in Aden was discouraged by the government. The situation with respect to the press was thus far more draconian than it was in Saudi Arabia, where the King permitted publication of at least one weekly newspaper given over to official news, although he rarely allowed foreign journalists to enter the country.

In Taʻizz, which lay in the coastal tropical fringe of Yemen, we were accommodated in a guest house provided by the Crown Prince. A chamberlain called to announce that I would be received promptly the next morning at nine because I had given notice of my intention to leave by eleven in order to reach Aden that same day. As nothing ever goes according to schedule in Yemen, I was not astonished when the hour of nine passed the next day with no sign of anyone to conduct me to the Crown Prince's palace. When nine-thirty came, I determined to lend myself no longer to the perpetual Yemeni game of cat-and-mouse. Accordingly I asked an attendant to inform His Royal Highness of my regret that I would be denied the pleasure of being received by him and asked that I be sent the police pass permitting my departure. I was not altogether surprised to be informed that the Crown Prince was waiting my pleasure to grant me audience.

Following my first visit to Yemen, Ambassador Jefferson Caffery asked what I considered my most notable accomplishment as minister to that country. I replied that the answer could not be simpler: six months after my return to Jidda and after a protracted exchange of notes I had succeeded in obtaining an official receipt for a truck which the American Government had presented as a gift to Yemen a year before the presentation of my credentials.

Happily I was able to count much more substantial and less farcical achievements later. Thus, I eventually persuaded the Yemen Government to permit the official visit to the United States of Prince Abdullah, the first ever paid by a Yemeni official. I also succeeded in inducing Yemen to make application for admission to the United Nations and to appoint a minister to Washington, as well as concluding other accords. My mission as first American Minister to Yemen thus resulted in an important breach in the century-old isolation of that country.

During the four years in which I was accredited to Yemen, I repeatedly endeavored to visit Marib, the ancient capital of the Queen of Sheba, lying on the edge of the desert in the northeast close by Saudi Arabia. Only two Europeans, archaeologists, had ever set eye on it, in the second half of the nineteenth century. Whenever I raised the subject of Marib with the Yemeni authorities, I was met with evasive replies.

The opportunity I had so long sought came in 1950. After patient overtures I obtained permission, in connection with an official visit to Imam Ahmed at Ta'izz, to fly there in my own plane, the first American aircraft to touch at Ta'izz. It was something of a risk as the primitive airstrip had been constructed on the sloping crest of a small hill in a narrow valley enclosed on every side by peaks rising several thousand feet high. I had, however, implicit confidence in my pilot, Jack Womack. We landed safely, but when we prepared to take off at the end of our stay of ten days Jack was not altogether happy.

The flight plan disclosed to the Yemenis was to fly north in a very short hop to San'a, where we were to stop for a few hours. I proposed to Jack that en route we make a diversion northeastward in the direction where we conjectured Marib to be and, if we found the ruins, to circle as low as possible for a good view and then to proceed to San'a. The delay should be no more than an hour, and we could always claim we had lost our way after quitting Ta'izz. Such an explanation was the more plausible in that no proper aerial maps existed of Yemen.

When Jack again surveyed the airstrip for our take-off on the morning of our departure, he shook his head. We were ten in the party with the crew, the runway was alarmingly short with a precipice at either end, and there was a cross wind. It seemed prudent to him to offload several hundred gallons of gasoline and to keep only the bare minimum needed to take us to Marib and San'a. The latter was close to Kamaran Island, where we could refuel. We held our breath until airborne and until we had surmounted the peaks which encompassed the primitive airport.

Soon our search for Marib began. Wide circling sweeps were made over an extensive area for an hour or more with no sign of our objective. We had but little to go on except the meager accounts of the city and its ancient ruins in the desert which were said to have been alongside an ancient rivercourse and dam, the breaking of which had inundated the Queen of Sheba's capital.

After a vain search of more than an hour Jack announced that our gasoline supply was running so low that it was imperative we head west for San'a. There was no identifiable landmark by which our position might be fixed. However, the Red Sea was due west of us and once there we would be able to obtain our bearings. Accordingly we reluctantly relinquished our quest of Marib and proceeded on a due westerly course. We had hardly done so when there was a shout from a member of our party. Scanning the horizon, he had espied an ancient site in the far distance slightly to the left of our course.

There was no mistaking it once we had arrived in its vicinity. A walled enclave on an eminence was evidently the comparatively modern town of Marib. Alongside it was a dry river bed across which could still be discerned the remains of the great dam which had served to store water for the area in antiquity. Spread out in the desert were the marble columns of the palaces of the Queen of Sheba, making identification unquestionable.

So short was our fuel by this time that we were unable to descend but had to content ourselves with one circle of the area from the height at which we were flying. During that time our photographer was busy taking the first pictures ever snapped of the historic and inaccessible site.[1] There could be no thought of landing at San'a before replenishing our fuel supply at Kamaran, to which we could practically coast. When we made our landing there was hardly a cup of gasoline remaining.

On hastily making our way back to San'a, which we reached at two o'clock, we found still assembled at the airport the Yemeni officials who had been awaiting us since early morning. They were far too intelligent to be taken in by our lame explanation that winds had diverted us off our course. They confided that reports had been received of our having been sighted at various points in the east. It was quite impossible, however, to draw from them any specific identification of the towns and villages over which we had passed; Yemenis prefer to mystify rather than enlighten a foreigner about their country.

If dealing with the people of Yemen required the exercise of more patience than was needed at any other time in my career, it was not without its entertaining side. Whether the Arabs concerned are Yemenis or Saudis, a foreigner needs to have infinite patience and a sense of humor and to avoid any least display of temper.

On the flight back, when stopping at Asmara, I was received by one of the King's sons residing there temporarily for his health. When I was presented to him, he failed to rise. Later when I expressed to one of his suite my distress that His Highness was suffering from an inflammation of his limbs, he was quite positive in his assurances that he suffered from no such disability. "You must be mistaken," I told him. "When I was introduced to the Prince this morning, he remained seated in his chair although his father, the King, a much older man, rose when receiving me in audience."

If one of the essential traits of a diplomat when dealing with the Arabs is imperturbability, equally important is that of administering a merited rebuke without giving offense. I was once about to take off in my plane from Jidda to keep an appointment with the King in Riyadh when I was halted by the Saudi airport authorities. They objected that they had received no clearance from the King for my visit. Instead of exhibiting any trace of annoyance, I calmly left the plane with my staff and returned to the embassy.

My first act was to send a telegram to the principal minister at the palace asking that he convey my regrets to the King for failing to keep my appointment. I was confident that the underling in charge at the Foreign Ministry would be expecting a vigorous protest on my part and that after reading a copy of my telegram, which would be relayed to him, he would be on the telephone offering me every facility.

That seemed to me too easy an out under the circumstances.

The modern city of Marib, Yemen, in 1950

By Command of His Imperial Majesty
Haile Sellassie I.
Emperor of Ethiopia

The A. D. C. to His Imperial Majesty has the honour to
request the attendance of *His Excellency the American Ambassador and Mrs. J. Rives Childs*
to a Reception at the Imperial Palace, *Old Gibbi,*
on *Monday* the *Fifth* of *May* 1952, at 8 p.m.
on the occasion of the Eleventh Anniversary of His Imperial Majesty's return to the capital.

R. S. V. P.
A. D. C. to H. I. M.   *Formal dress and decorations.*

An invitation received from His Imperial Majesty Haile Selassie I to a reception at the Palace on May 5, 1952

Emperor Haile Selassie at the time of the federation of Eritrea with Ethiopia in September and October of 1952

Accordingly, I gave orders that I was not accepting any telephone calls. I then ordered the embassy launch to be readied and announced that I was going fishing for the day.

On my return late that afternoon I was informed that the Foreign Ministry had been endeavoring to telephone me ever since my departure and that I had been asked to call back urgently. There was no hurry; I would let the pot simmer and wait until the ranking official telephoned again. When he did so, he informed me that a most regrettable mistake had been made. No one in Jidda had been informed of my appointment with His Majesty; an urgent telegram had been received from the King inquiring when I might be expected. "It depends on you," I calmly answered. "May we say that you intend to leave tomorrow morning?" "You may, provided you intend to place no obstruction in my way," I observed in my mildest voice.

Since my departure from Yemen, Soviet Russia is reported to have gained the influence we once enjoyed there until it was lost because of our support of the Zionists in the Arab-Jewish conflict in the Near East. More lately there has been an intrusion of Egyptians. I do not look with alarm at a Soviet or any other penetration. In the Yemenis, Russians and Egyptians alike will find their match. The Yemenis are more than their masters in intrigue and in the pursuit of Fabian tactics. I doubt that the Soviets will find them anything like as entertaining as I did. The Egyptians are closer in blood, but the Yemenis are capable of outfoxing any people within the range of my experience.

Upon the termination of my four years as Ambassador to Saudi Arabia and as Minister to Yemen, I was named Ambassador to Ethiopia.

As one of the oldest Christian nations and, until recently, the only independent native state in Africa, Ethiopia is a country of astonishing contrasts, with extensive fertile land and forests on the high plateau and a tropical region in its south and east. Only since the beginning of the reign of Emperor Haile Selassie has order been introduced among formerly independent or semi-independent tribes and a strong central government established.

From remote times even before the Christian era Ethiopia was linked with Yemen and Egypt. It was actually a province of Egypt under the eighteenth dynasty. About the eleventh century B.C. it became independent, and eventually, through a turn of fortune's wheel, it gained the mastery of Egypt, over which it exercised sway for some four centuries. It was from the ancient Coptic Church of Egypt that Christianity was introduced into Ethiopia in the fourth century, and it was this church which, until recent years, asserted its right to name the Ethiopian archbishop, known as the Abuna.

The fortunes of the two countries are inextricably linked by nature. It is the heavy precipitation on the Ethiopian highlands every summer which feeds Lake Tana and the Blue Nile; in turn this unites with the White Nile near Khartoum to form the river whose waters sustain Egyptian agriculture. So fixed is the schedule of rainfall that every year the Emperor issues a proclamation anticipating the end of the rainy season and fixing a date for the appropriate celebration.

To Yemen, Ethiopia owes the source of part of its population, an immigration which took place across the Red Sea from Asia to Africa in remote antiquity. According to tradition which is so far recognized that it is invoked in official acts, the Emperor is descended from a son of King Solomon and a queen of Sheba, of Marib. The most popular souvenir offered to visitors is a series of scenes painted on a canvas roll depicting the nuptial foregathering of Solomon's son and the queen. The pictures are wholly devoid of any erotic element but their naïveté is exceedingly comic.

It has always been my view that the worst introduction to a country is to enter it by airplane. For this reason we chose to make the journey of 436 miles by the French-administered railway, departing from Djibouti on the Red Sea and terminating in Addis Ababa. A sleeping car is on the evening train from Djibouti which reaches Diredawa the following morning. There, after a stop for breakfast, one changes to a diesel-powered coach which slowly ascends from the lowlands to Addis Ababa at 8,000 feet on the high plateau. The railway passes through the typical scrub bush of an African landscape with heavily forested mountains looming in the distance. An added attraction is the wild life to be seen scampering for cover as the train passes. So rich is the fauna that some time later, when the Emperor gave me permission to shoot in his game preserve, the sight of literally hundreds of dik-diks, resembling small gazelles, gazelles themselves, oryxes, elands, and the many other antlered game animals with which the country abounds took from me all desire to fire my gun and be guilty of sheer massacre.

Addis Ababa, capital of Ethiopia, lying spread out in the saddle of a mountain, resembles in some respects the site of Darjeeling in the Himalayas. The climate was in sharp contrast with the trying heat from which we had suffered for four years in Saudi Arabia, where I had rarely been free of prickly heat until the introduction of airconditioning. A very comfortable and commodious embassy set in a large park of eucalyptus trees, one of the most distinguishing features of central Ethiopia, afforded us an existence far less primitive and stark than that of Jidda. If the natives of the interior pursued a way of life quite as simple and patriarchal as Saudi Arabians, there were numerous highly refined Ethiopians in Addis to make life agreeable.

The capital was an extraordinary contrast of the old and new. Even the most cultivated Ethiopians were addicted to raw meat, as well as to the choicest dishes of the West. *Tukels* or round thatched conical huts, resembling the *rondevels* of central Africa, in which natives made their homes, were ranged alongside the most modern buildings. In the center of the city, which was undergoing rapid modernization, caged lions were maintained as symbols of the Emperor's title of "conquering lion of Judah," while at night hyenas roamed the streets and served as natural garbage collectors.

Archaeological remains at Aksum, of Yemeni origin, reflected the close ties which had once existed between Yemen and Ethiopia. At Gondar imposing castles resembling the medieval fortresses of Europe offered relics of that Prester John who had appealed, in the sixteenth century, for aid against the Moslems when Portuguese influence extended over a large part of the coast line of Africa and Asia. Italian roads on which Mussolini had expended some two hundred million dollars, remained as evidence of Fascism's folly in the invasion of the country in 1935 and its occupancy until 1941. Curiously, the Italians, even in their brief sojourn, had left such an impress that their language remained the lingua franca even in the most remote regions.

I was privileged to have many interesting talks with the Emperor, whom I found more formal than Ibn Saud and much more reserved. Emperor Haile Selassie is a handsome man of slight build. He is well acquainted with English but prefers to speak French. The impression he conveyed to me was of a man of great inner reserves of strength. His words were chosen with studied deliberation, and his thoughts were communicated with great economy of speech. A natural gentleness was reflected in his manners, belied by piercing dark eyes reflecting a will of steel. No more eloquent and moving appeal was ever made to the League of Nations than he made at Geneva in the face of the Italian threat to his country—a threat to which the Great Powers chose to close their eyes and ears.

The Emperor's passion was the education of his country's youth, and great strides had been made in the realization of this objective. I took special pains to visit some of the schools and was greatly impressed by the ability of the school children to acquire at a very early age a knowledge of English, the official language of the country along with Amharic, the indigenous tongue of Ethiopians. In a discussion of education with the Emperor he remarked:

I am more interested for the moment in providing my people with technical training than with purely cultural knowledge in the arts and sciences. What we need most of all to begin with are technicians, men capable of dealing with machinery and of repairing motor vehicles and generators. We have no place for the present for a plethora of college graduates incapable of using their hands.

In Egypt I had seen the illogic of an overemphasis on higher education, with the turning out of college graduates in such numbers that insufficient jobs were available for them. The Emperor seemed determined that, if possible, Ethiopia should be spared the unbalance with which other countries were being increasingly plagued.

My work was anticlimactic after the challenging five years in Tangier and four in Saudi Arabia. Ethiopia was in many respects a diplomatic backwater. Its relations with the United States were so friendly that there were few problems of any complexity. The Emperor had very wisely refused to be drawn into committing himself to any one power to the exclusion of others. To the British he turned for educators, to the Swedish for organization of the police and the Air Force, to the Dutch for financial advice, and to the French for maintenance of the one railway line. On the United States he relied for personnel to operate the Ethiopian Air Lines and for experts from the Bureau of Public Roads to advise in the overhauling of the highway system. During my tenure of office of less than two years, I prepared the ground for a military agreement, including a training program, concluded a treaty of friendship as well as a Point Four program, and otherwise spent my time in traveling by car about the country to familiarize myself with its great variety of scenery and peoples.

Such travel was necessarily confined to certain main roads radiating from Addis Ababa. Farther afield communications became increasingly difficult and impractical, as well as dangerous owing to the presence of unfriendly primitive tribes. This was especially true of the south in the vicinity of the Sudan and Kenya borders. On a trip through Soddu one member of the embassy staff encountered stark-naked Ethiopians armed only with spears. They were pagans who worshiped trees, waterfalls, and even snakes. The snakes most held in reverence were pythons. The Borani practice is to keep the snakes in a cave, where they are fed sheep and goats. Once a year they are transported in baskets, by camel, to a remote spot in the lava fields south of Moga on the Kenya border. There live children are fed to them. The families of the children deem the sacrifice of their children a great honor.

In the variety of its people and their distinctive customs Ethiopia is in a sense an ethnological museum. It is also rich in archaeological remains of a primitive character. Travelers have reported near Neghelli the presence of a series of oblong monoliths about two feet square by eight feet high, the tops of which are pointed. They are spaced at fairly even intervals of about 1,000 yards. Another series, of dressed red granite, about four feet wide, two feet thick, and originally some fifty feet long, of oval shape, have been found between Neghelli and Adola, center of the gold mining industry. There is every indication that they had once been erect and had fallen, breaking into four roughly equal segments. No inscriptions or designs are observable on the exposed parts. In the rear of the American Embassy in Addis Ababa, within the garden, is a series of stone monoliths which appear to have been cut to a uniform size and half-buried in the earth in strict alignment, the exposed parts measuring roughly some ten feet in length. Neither these nor the other monoliths to which reference has been made seem to be the product of any geological process. Several hundred, lying in a line, have been reported between Uondo and the northern shore of Lake Abaya. These bear carvings believed to be symbols of fertility. The stones themselves are said to be of a phallic nature although no remnant of phallic worship is now practiced by natives of the area. These details were communicated to me by Mr. Charles Reynolds after a 1952 journey made at considerable risk. Some of the monoliths described may have a certain analogy with the ancient menhirs found in Brittany.

Aside from Gondar and Aksum, which are among the most interesting cities historically in Ethiopia, I was interested in paying a visit to Harar in the southwest. This city had only been a part of Ethiopia since 1887. In outward appearance it is far more Arabian than Ethiopian, having been settled by Arabs from Yemen. It was long a terra incognita to foreigners. As might be expected, the translator of *The Arabian Nights* and dashing explorer, Sir Richard Francis Burton, was the first European to set foot in Harar, to which he gained access in 1854, as he had to Mecca, disguised as an Arab.

Not only did Harar offer this romantic appeal but it had further interest as the residence from 1880 to 1891 of that extraordinary figure Arthur Rimbaud, one of the greatest poets of the nineteenth century. At the age of nineteen, after dazzling littérateurs with his poetry, he had renounced his precocious gifts for reasons which have never been fathomed and embarked upon a life of adventure, which led him to Aden and Ethiopia and, finally, to an untimely death at Marseilles in 1891 at the age of thirty-seven. In Harar, Rimbaud was known as a trader in coffee, ivory, gold, and even slaves. Not one person was left in the town who had either known him or heard his name mentioned.

If I had comparatively little of moment in the way of diplomatic activity with which to occupy myself in Ethiopia, there were nevertheless compensations. An action on which I look back with especial satisfaction is one concerned with a request from an association of American motion picture producers that I endeavor to have Ethiopia lift the ban on the showing of gangster films. There may be some question as to how far these have contributed to juvenile delinquency, but there can be no dispute that they have distorted the picture of American life in the eyes of foreigners.

With the letter in my hand I called on the Minister of Finance in charge of film censorship. As I read it to him his brows visibly contracted. When I had finished, I stated: "Mr. Minister, my visit is not for the purpose of complying with the request I have just read but to offer, not as ambassador but in my personal capacity, an expression of my complete sympathy with the ban and of my hope that there will be no relaxation of it." In acknowledging the letter of the Association of American Motion Picture Producers, I expressed the view that no useful purpose would be served by raising the issue. This episode made the Minister of Finance so firm a friend that my failure to intercede on behalf of American film interests to attain an objective which could only be prejudicial to the United States had the constructive consequence of creating good will for my government.

Ethiopians are a highly conservative people and they looked askance at certain of the unceremonious ways of Americans and other foreigners in their midst. The embassy compound comprised a series of attractive bungalows for the housing of the senior personnel and their wives. On arriving in Ethiopia, the wives often appeared in the compound in slacks and even shorts, to the scandal of the Ethiopians to whom they were visible. As soon as this came to my attention, I published a notice forbidding the use of such garb outside the home. The next day I was waited on by a deputation of American wives. Their spokeswoman found it difficult to conceal her indignation that an American male should dare to dictate to American women what they should wear.

"I am charged," I replied, "with the responsibility of safeguarding American interests in this country and of conserving our prestige and good name. Addis Ababa is not a suburban town in the United States. Here a woman who wears slacks or shorts demeans herself in the eyes of Ethiopians as well as of other foreigners. You may wear what you like when you are in your home, but I must have something to say when the name of the United States and its reputation are at stake."

"Suppose we refuse to conform?" one of the girls asked.

"In that case I shall see that the husband of the recalcitrant wife is recalled, which will mean her departure also. Any other questions?"

And that was the last of the slacks and shorts issue.

My troubles were not confined to the gentler sex.

When Eritrea, once an Italian possession on the Red Sea, became a part of Ethiopia in 1952, I recommended that we send a warship to Massawa as a courtesy to the Emperor in honor of the occasion. On the appearance of the admiral he readily fell in with my suggestion that he invite the Emperor and Empress to a luncheon aboard his ship.

In Addis Ababa we made up a caravan to proceed overland to Asmara to assist at the ceremony to which the diplomatic corps had been invited. In the absence of suitable hotels en route we took our own camping equipment. The trip offered an excellent opportunity to view the grandiose mountain scenery with which the plateau abounds and to test the superb road built by the Italians to connect the Ethiopian capital and the former capital of Eritrea. The stupendous labor expended by the Italians on this one road which traversed one mountain after another evidenced the degree of permanence which the Italians ascribed to their conquest of the country.

In Asmara my military attaché and I called in the admiral's aide to discuss the arrangements for the luncheon. I stated that, of course, the Emperor and Empress would act as host and hostess on board the American vessel. The aide was quite outraged by the idea. I explained patiently that in accordance with universal protocol when an ambassador received a sovereign the latter was given the place of host even though an embassy was as much national territory as a naval vessel.

The aide would have none of it. "The admiral will never agree," he repeated stubbornly.

"How long have you been in the navy?" the military attaché inquired sharply.

"Three years."

"I have been in the army for twenty and the ambassador in the foreign service for almost thirty. My advice to you is to listen and to report to the admiral with no further comment on your part."

At the luncheon the admiral was seated on the right of the Empress and the admiral's wife on the right of the Emperor.

Happily, not all of my work was as inconsequential as this. By a curious quirk of fate a problem which had concerned me from the outset of my career in 1923, in Palestine, continued to be with me until the end thirty years later.

In common with other missions in the Near East I was requested by the Department of State in 1952 to comment on the lack of support accorded the United States by the Arab states during the sixth session of the General Assembly of the United Nations. In my reply I stated:

United States support of Israel has undermined the confidence and trust which we once enjoyed in the Arab world. Pious and platitudinous professions of interest in that world are not likely to change the distrust in which we are now held by the majority of Arabs. The Arabs cannot forget that on the eve of the creation of the State of Israel the most explicit assurances were given their governments of our intentions to take Arab interests into account, assurances which were shortly thereafter disregarded. Nor can they forget the assurances given by President Roosevelt to King Ibn Saud that no measures would be taken affecting Arab interests without consultation. Such consultations in most instances have taken the form of the presentation to them of faits accomplis.

The Arabs are told that we intend to treat henceforth the Arabs and Jews alike but this equality is interpreted by us as an equal division of grants between the Israeli and Arab world when there is no comparable proportion in either the number of states involved nor in the number of peoples concerned. They hear the Vice President declaring that Israel is an island of democracy in a sea of despotism and they learn through their own experience that there is no equality in the treatment of news by the American press in matters relating to Israel and those relating to the Arabs. Until the United States treats Arabs and Israelis officially and unofficially on a footing of real and not professed equality we have little likelihood of restoring even a modicum of the trust and confidence in us which was at one time universal in the Arab world.

In a way it was my swan song. I was highly gratified by numerous expressions of concurrence in the conclusion on the part of colleagues to whom it was sent; I would have been more gratified if it had struck a responsive chord in Washington.

Epilogue

In 1952, at the age of fifty-nine and with some six years still remaining before involuntary retirement, I came after long thought to the decision to take the initiative in bringing my diplomatic career to a close. In this I was moved by many motives. On leaving Saudi Arabia, I had hoped for a European assignment. When I wrote to George McGee and made the suggestion, he replied that he, in his capacity as Assistant Secretary of State for Near Eastern Affairs, would not oppose my use of any political influence I might have to that end. I answered that after more than twenty-five years in the service I did not intend to resort for the first time to such means in obtaining an assignment.

When my request was not acted upon and I was assigned to Ethiopia, I indulged in no self-pity nor did I entertain any feeling of grievance. I had long since recognized that I was far from being an ideal diplomatic agent. I know of no better summary of the qualities befitting a diplomat than that once offered by the sometime Italian diplomat Jacques Casanova de Seingalt:

In general, the real superiority of the mind, study, science, simple and quiet tastes are qualities little esteemed in a diplomat. They only serve to close the door to the discharge of his duties. I know more than one of high rank who has owed his disgrace entirely to his merit. Governments always prefer to have under their hands blind and docile instruments.[2]

I was anything but a "blind and docile instrument." I had never hesitated to express my point of view. An officer who gains a reputation for persistence in making his views known, particularly on measures the lines of which have already been formulated, comes in the end inevitably to make a nuisance of himself. I was aware that I fell within that category. Independence of mind—and I write without any intended irony—is a quality which detracts seriously from the value of a diplomat. His not to reason why; what is essential is that, with no interposition of his own personality, he carry out blindly the instructions of his government. That is the guiding principle of the ideal officer. There are none who come closer to the ideal than Soviet diplomats. It may only be a question of time before American foreign service officers are equally self-effacing and obedient. My temperament was such that I was incapable of assuming such a role.

There were still other considerations which persuaded me to retire. I made a balance sheet of my career. From 1923 to 1941 I had practically marked time. True, I had built up a certain amount of good will for the United States, but good will is as evanescent as smoke. In Morocco, in 1942, I might have made an important contribution by averting some 3,000 casualties there on the occasion of our landings. That opportunity was denied me. In the Near East, where I had spent my life and where I, along with all other chiefs of missions to Arab states, had warned against the partiality we had shown to Israel, there had been a progressive deterioration both in our relations with the Arab world as well as in Arab-Israeli relations. Our warnings had counted for nothing.

My conclusion was that I was more competent to direct my own activities in constructive pursuits than was the United States Government. A casual incident tipped my hand. I telegraphed Washington suggesting that it would be useful for me to go to Rome to confer with Ambassador James C. Dunn on a problem in which we were both involved. He concurred, but the State Department thought otherwise. That settled it for me. If my judgment carried so little weight, it was more than clear that every day I spent in office was a waste of my time and a quite useless expenditure of the government in paying my salary.

There was one final contributing factor. I had enjoyed a life of relative pomp and power. To me there was a deep moral satisfaction in voluntarily renouncing it. That I was correct in this estimate was proved abundantly in the inner strength I acquired after my return to private life.

So it was that I offered my resignation to become effective at the close of President Truman's term of office. Early in 1953 I took leave of Ethiopia and of the foreign service. It was a painful moment to bid farewell to my staff and to a lifetime of service with the government. My wife had preceded me to Nice upon the death of her mother. There I headed and there we quickly found an apartment in a park, with privacy and quiet and a view of the sea and mountains. For the first time in thirty years I was free to do and write and speak as I pleased.

Nice 1953–1968

NOTES

Chapter I

[1] I once intimated to Friedman that it was difficult to understand how a man of his intelligence could take seriously the task assigned to him. Friedman shrugged his shoulders as if suggesting that it was his livelihood and that if a millionaire was willing to pay for being humored it was not for him to dispute his idiosyncrasies. In 1957 he and Elizebeth Smith, whom he had married, published *The Shakespearean Ciphers Examined* (Cambridge University Press), in which they effectively demolished the Baconian cipher thesis. He eventually became a key figure in the National Security Agency and is one of the few persons to have been awarded by Congress a grant *ex dono* of $100,000 for his cryptographic services to the government.

[2] Many French military historians hold that Painvin's remarkable gifts may have been a determining factor in bringing the war to a successful conclusion in 1918. One of the most somber days of that conflict was May 27, 1918, when, after advancing again almost to the Marne, the Germans seemed to have Paris within their grasp. With a dearth of French reserves the crucial question became where the next attack might be launched. In a German message of June 1 which Painvin deciphered on the third there was clear indication that it would take place in the vicinity of Remaugies. As a result, when it came on the ninth, Mangin's forces, which had been hastily assembled to oppose it, were not only successful in this but in undertaking a counteroffensive, which proved to be one of the turning points of the war.

[3] After his demobilization he opened, ostensibly, a commercial code-compiling agency in New York as a cover for his more serious and confidential cryptographic activities, which were supported by funds of the State and War Departments. His greatest coup was the reading of the Japanese code during the Washington Naval Conference. When Henry L. Stimson took office as Secretary of State in 1929 and learned of Yardley's work of reading the secret communications of foreign governments, he ordered its cessation with the observation that "gentlemen do not read each other's mail." To earn money Yardley wrote and published *The American Black Chamber* (Indianapolis, 1931) about his secret activities—to the great embarrassment of the government. Some interesting details of Yardley's tragic and inglorious end, involving drug addiction and betrayal of his country, may be found in Ladislas Farago's *The Broken Seal* (New York, 1967), pp. 396, 398.

Farago seems unaware of a fact on which I can throw some light. In 1938 or 1939, while serving at the State Department, I received a telephone call from the military attaché of the Chinese Embassy. Without volunteering the specific purpose, he expressed a desire to pay an unobtrusive call on me at my home. When I received him that evening in Alexandria, he inquired about Yardley's qualifications as a cryptographer inasmuch as he was applying for a job in that capacity with the Chinese Government, then in conflict with Japan. I told him what I knew of Yardley's brilliant accomplishments. Shortly thereafter Yardley wrote me that he had received the appointment at a handsome salary ($12,000 or $15,000 and expenses, as I recall) and was leaving soon for China. I received one or two letters from him and then broke off the correspondence and never saw him again.

[4] Cf. the New York *Times* of May 14, 1920, an editorial in the same newspaper on May 15, and the full text of the report on May 16.

Chapter II

[1] In Kazan he married Princess Chegodayiva, from whom he was later divorced when he was unable to obtain an exit visa for her. During the depression he fell upon hard times, and heavy drinking caused his death. In Kazan he would often remark wistfully to me: "You need have no concern about the future, but everything looks dark for me." With his charm, quick mind, and generous nature he deserved better of fate.

[2] A play by Charles Klein based on stories by Montague Glass and produced in New York on August 16, 1913.

[3] I lost touch with him until, some thirty years later, a distinguished American painter, Murray Bewley, gave me news of him in Nice.

[4] Governments are notoriously lacking in gratitude and there need be no astonishment if the memory of our work finds no echo today among Soviet officials. Yet there must be gratitude on the part of the many still alive whose existence we preserved in 1921–23 with our food.

[5] John afterward played a notable part in the North African landings in 1942, while I was stationed in Tangier. Like me he spends half of every year in Nice, where we try to persuade ourselves we still have something of our old fire. He was best man at my wedding in Leningrad in 1922, and forty-two years later he stood by my side in Nice when my wife was buried there.

Chapter III

[1] U.S. Department of State, *Papers Relating to the Foreign Relations of the United States, 1918, Russia* (Washington, 1931–32) II, 477–84.

Chapter IV

[1] The King-Crane Report (formally entitled *Report of the American Section of the International Commission on Mandates in Turkey*) has been published in *For. Rel. U.S., The Paris Peace Conference, 1919* (Washington, 1942–47), XII, 745–863. Cf. also Harry N. Howard, *The King-Crane Commission* (Beirut, 1963).

[2] I did not neglect even publications of the Communist International. On reading an observation by the Berlin correspondent of the *Manchester Guardian Weekly* of an exceptionally well-informed periodical known as *Inter-*

national Press Correspondence, I succeeded after great difficulty in obtaining its address and entering a subscription. I continued to receive it in Egypt and Iran until Hitler's dissolution of the Communist party in Germany terminated its life. The economic analyses which it published were of outstanding quality, with due allowance for its Marxist bias, of course.

Chapter VI

[1] *The Adventures of Hajji Baba of Ispahan,* by James J. Morier, was first published in London in 1824 and has been frequently reprinted.

[2] *War and Revolution in Asiatic Russia* (London, 1918), cited in Henry Filmer (*pseud.* of J. Rives Childs), *The Pageant of Persia* (Indianapolis, 1936), p. viii.

[3] The inspiration of my study was Georgii Agabekov's *Ogpu, the Russian Secret Terror* (New York, 1931), an account of Soviet machinations in Iran. A copy of this work was among the books given me by Charles R. Crane (see p. 53).

[4] Soviet political penetration in the Near East prior to the Second World War was severely handicapped by the refusal of most countries to accept Russian diplomatic representation. Persia, Afghanistan, and Turkey were rare exceptions where Soviet missions were to be found.

[5] Pp. 357–59.

Chapter VII

[1] My despatch, No. 377, of October 21, 1935, and the Department's acknowledgment of November 21, 1935, File No. 765.84/2345. If I cite these and other official reports from time to time, it is to protect myself from the charge to which memorialists are subject that the prescience they sometimes claim cannot be supported by the facts. I was, of course, wide of the mark at times, but generally under circumstances which have no particular interest.

[2] My despatch, No. 501, of June 1, 1932, under the minister's signature, from the American Legation in Cairo.

[3] Page 96 of the novel published in Indianapolis under the pseudonym Henry Filmer.

Chapter VIII

[1] Cf. *For. Rel. U.S., 1940,* III, 838.

[2] Although the initial draft was begun at the end of October, it was eventually dated November 12, 1940. Cf. *ibid.,* II, 622.

[3] For a memorandum of the conversation, see *ibid.,* pp. 602–4.

Chapter IX

[1] Although there is a wealth of published material on the Allied landings in Algeria and the diplomatic and political developments arising therefrom

in that particular area, that concerning Morocco is singularly scanty. Even Robert Murphy in his *Diplomat among Warriors* (Garden City, N.Y., 1964) touches very lightly and sketchily on the events and their aftermath in that country.

[2] Cf. *For. Rel. U.S.*, *1941*, III, 555.

[3] President Roosevelt was so far impressed by the possibilities opened up by the Orgaz negotiations that he took a personal interest in them (cf. *For. Rel. U.S.*, *1942*, IV, 439–86).

[4] The White House was not equally successful in its desire to keep principal American foreign service officers in French North Africa in ignorance of the prospective landings. I learned later of a telegram from Roosevelt to Murphy shortly before the operation began that under no circumstances was I or other State Department officers in French North Africa to be given any prior intimation of a project with which I had already been acquainted for five months.

[5] Cf. my telegram No. 563 of November 8, 1942 (*ibid.*, IV, 511–12).

[6] Cf. *For. Rel. U.S.*, *1942*, II, 308–10.

[7] When his trial took place in Paris in 1956, he sent word to ask if I would be willing to testify in his behalf. In the belief that we bore some responsibility for his fate, I readily acceded. To begin with, I made available to him an account I had already written of the events as abridged in the present chapter. After referring it to his attorney, he returned it with the observation that he himself could not have described his reaction to the events recounted more correctly.

[8] New York, 1948, pp. 652–53.

[9] It is clear that there was no lack of intelligence reports so far as Tangier was concerned. What is obvious is that these were either ignored or discounted.

[10] An examination of certain studies of French historians and memorialists, including in particular Admiral Paul Auphan's *Les Grimaces de l'histoire*, has disclosed the curious background of the telegram. After some earnest discussion on the receipt in Vichy on November 13 of Noguès' telegram from Algiers, Marshal Pétain expressed approval of Noguès' report and of his recommendation that the power entrusted to him should be transferred to Darlan. Auphan was thereupon charged by Pétain with drafting a reply to this effect, which was to be shown to Laval before being sent. "However, M. Laval—while being in accord, so he stated, on the whole—did not wish to respond without being assured beforehand of German acquiescence, which rendered the matter impossible." In the absence of Laval's countersignature, Auphan took it on himself to send to Darlan by a secret cipher, known to but few, a preliminary acknowledgment. It was this text which Noguès had shown me.

[11] For Roosevelt's defense of the choice of Darlan, see *Department of State Bulletin*, VII (1942), 935, or newspapers for Nov. 17 or 18, 1942. For Eisenhower's account, see pp. 104–11 of his book (Garden City, N.Y., 1943). For Stalin's acceptance, see Churchill's *The Second World War*, IV, *The Hinge of Fate* (London, 1951), p. 598. Although he justified the decision in his memoirs, Churchill's initial reaction was one of misgivings. On November 17, 1942, he telegraphed Roosevelt that "we must not overlook the serious political injury which may be done to our cause . . . by the feeling that we are ready to make terms with local Quislings. Darlan has an odious record. . . . A permanent arrangement with Darlan . . . would not be understood by the great

masses of ordinary people whose simple loyalties are our strength" (cf. *For. Rel. U.S.*, 1942, II, 445–46).

[12] Was the instinctive reaction of public opinion unsound? However that may be, it is possible to argue that there was another way out. So far as the vexed problem of legitimacy was concerned, that had been solved by the designation of Noguès as Pétain's representative. Yet the availability of Noguès, untouched by any taint of collaboration, never seems to have been considered. A French historian of these events and also a senior French diplomat have told me their conviction that Darlan was the only French personality available in French North Africa who possessed the requisite authority to exercise command and thereby to ensure French cooperation with the Allies. Yet Darlan's influence with his own fleet was so negligible that it ignored his appeal to lift anchor at Toulon and join him in Algiers. As to Roosevelt's contention that the deal with Darlan had been made to save lives and gain time in the mopping up of Algeria and Morocco, the fact was that there had been a suspension of arms in Algeria as early as November 9 and in Morocco on November 11. The designation of Darlan was made after all resistance there had ceased. That the decision to invest Darlan with power was made by harassed and perplexed American representatives in Algiers, bewildered by the complexity of the political problems facing them, is evident; that there was no other course open is questionable. One element admits of no argument—the moral damage done the Allied cause.

[13] The meeting had its inception in a proposal of the Spanish Minister for Foreign Affairs to the American Ambassador in Madrid that General Eisenhower as commander in chief of American forces in North Africa should call on Orgaz. As it was difficult for General Eisenhower to absent himself from the theater of war, Patton was designated to act in his stead (cf. *For. Rel. U.S.*, *1942*, IV, 524–26, 528–30).

[14] I was as heedless of Algiers when it sought to concern itself with problems which I took to be outside its province. The suggestion having been made that the reports of all foreign service officers in French North Africa be subject to military censorship, the more effectively to control the expression of opinions directed to the Department of State regarding the troubled course of events, I raised two questions with Washington: one, whether it was intended to apply to the reports of American consular officials only or of all those within the area of Allied occupation and, if the latter, the possible reaction of the foreign offices concerned; and, two, the assuredly adverse reaction of American public opinion if such a measure became known. No more was ever heard of it.

[15] New York: Macmillan, 1946, p. 241.

Chapter X

[1] I knew something about the creation of the Lawrence legend. One Sunday in 1918 I was having lunch with friends at the American Officers' Club in London when a war correspondent, asking to join us, introduced himself as Lowell Thomas, then quite unknown. What impressed me at the time was his ability to dramatize the simplest fact. He told us he had just returned from the Near East with what he believed to be one of the great stories of the

war—about a chap named T. E. Lawrence. Two years later I returned to London where Lowell Thomas was holding the British spellbound by his lecture on "Lawrence of Arabia." Lawrence was undoubtedly a very remarkable character. However, I have often been moved to speculate how much the Lawrence legend owed to Lowell Thomas.

[2] *The Forrestal Diaries*, ed. Walter Millis, with the collaboration of E. S. Duffield (New York, 1951), p. 346.

[3] P. 440.

[4] Written several years before the Israeli-Arab war in 1967.

[5] Since the accession of King Feisal that sovereign is understood to have introduced notable and promising reforms in Saudi Arabian finances. Many wasteful expenditures have been eliminated and greater funds are devoted to productive public works.

Chapter XI

[1] André Malraux has claimed to have flown over Marib in 1934 and to have taken aerial photographs of the site (*Antimémoires*, Paris: Gallimard, 1967), but the claims have been disputed. The descriptions he gives of both the flight and of Marib are vague. A review of the book in the *Times Literary Supplement* of January 11, 1968, found it in part fictional, with "high spots of mystification."

[2] *Mémoires* (Paris: Flammarion, [n.d.]), VI, 317.

INDEX

Foreign Service Farewell

was composed, printed, and bound by
Kingsport Press, Inc., Kingsport, Tennessee.
The paper is Warren's Olde Style
and the type is Janson.
Design is by Edward G. Foss.